W9-BNG-522

# Marketing in the Groundswell

# Marketing in the Groundswell

## Charlene Li and Josh Bernoff

Harvard Business Press

Boston, Massachusetts

No part of this publication may be reproduced, stored in or introduced into
a retrieval system, or transmitted, in any form, or by any means (electronic,
mechanical, photocopying, recording, or otherwise), without the prior
permission of the publisher. Requests for permission should be directed to
permissions@hbsp.harvard.edu, or mailed to Permissions, Harvard Business
School Publishing, 60 Harvard Way, Boston, Massachusetts 02163.

Library-of-Congress cataloging information available
ISBN  978-1-4221-2980-7

The paper used in this publication meets the requirements of the American
National Standard for Permanence of Paper for Publications and Documents
in Libraries and Archives Z39.48-1992.

# Table of Contents

# Introduction

Since *Groundswell* was published in April of 2008, two things have happened.

The global economy has gone into the dumper. And at the same time, marketers have fallen in love with social technologies.

From my vantage point at Forrester Research, I've watched organizations as diverse as Home Depot, IBM, and the Spanish bank BBVA embrace this new way of relating to customers. Why? Because it taps into the powerful, emotional relationships people have with brands and with each other. Plus, in these economic times, it's not only effective, it's *cost-effective*. Even as marketers cut back on expenses like advertising, they're continuing to invest in social technologies.

Here's the proof: in December 2008, amid all the stock market dives and layoffs, we surveyed 145 marketers. These marketers came from both consumer and B2B companies, ranging from 250 employees to more than 20,000. Forty-three percent had marketing budgets of at least \$10 million. Most were already pursuing social technology applications for marketing, and of those, 95 percent were planning to maintain or increase their investments, right in the teeth of the recession.

Most of these investments were modest; three-quarters were budgeted at \$100,000 or less. But they were growing. Social networking spending was increasing. Blogging spending was up. User-generated content spending was on the rise. In nearly every category, if marketers were using a social application for marketing, they planned to maintain or increase spending (see figure 1). Why? Because social applications work, and they're far cheaper than most other forms of marketing.

With this level of enthusiasm, I knew it was a good idea to create this smaller, focused edition of *Groundswell* just for marketers. The *groundswell*, as we originally defined it, is a social trend in which people use technologies to get the things they need from each other instead of from companies. *Marketing in the Groundswell* concentrates on how marketers can tap into the power of social networks, blogs, user-generated video, communities, ratings and reviews, and the whole panoply of online phenomena. This book includes chapters 5, 6, and 7 of the original, larger edition—the chapters focused on market

FIGURE 1

# How marketers plan to spend their money

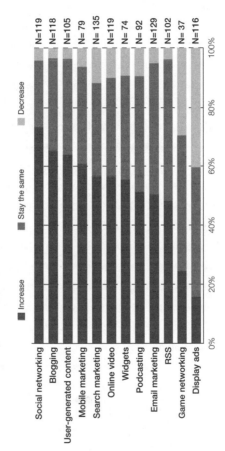

*Source:* Q4 2008 Forrester Global Social Media Planning Online Survey.

Base: 145 global interactive marketers at companies with 250+ employees who use each channel.

research, marketing, and spreading word-of-mouth among your best customers.

Think you're ready to learn about this way of marketing? Start by admitting that you're no longer in charge. People will talk about your brand, frequently in ways that won't be comfortable to see. Johnson & Johnson experienced this firsthand in November 2008 when it posted a video about how moms who wear their baby in a sling do it to be fashionable, despite the pain—so they should take Motrin to get over it. Thousands of moms who felt wearing their babies was more than a fashion statement displayed their anger and contempt for Motrin in blogs, on the short-messaging social application Twitter, and even in their own satirical YouTube videos. And this was over a weekend! By the time J&J got around to posting an apology, the damage had been done; a *New York Times* blog post had appeared about the uprising and product-critical videos were among the top Google search results on Motrin.

If you don't have the stomach for this, put this book down and then run and hide. But unfortunately, you'll find that not participating doesn't protect you from the groundswell—it only makes it harder to figure out how to respond when something like the Motrin moms uprising hits your company. If you build a strategy for connecting with your customers, not only can you accomplish marketing goals like increasing awareness, stimulating word of mouth, generating leads, and boosting sales, but you'll have both the knowledge and the tools to respond if a few of your customers decide to turn on you.

The other thing you should know is: *you can do this*. In the year since *Groundswell* was published, I have seen hundreds of ordinary marketers adopt groundswell ideas and build strategies around them. When we ran a workshop for the senior management at Wal-Mart, ten tables of executives came up with good ideas around everything from sustainability to employee connections, and even the table full of lawyers generated an impressive social networking idea. I watched a room full of credit card marketers come up with creative ways to energize their different customer segments. At one of the world's leading manufacturers of replacement hip joints, marketers came up with plans for how to reach both fifty-year-olds in pain and orthopedic surgeons. I saw that marketers really *do* know their customers, and if you give them permission to reach those customers in a new and effective way, they're happy to run with it.

The three chapters in this book show how to build these applications and how to measure their results. You'll hear not only from the marketers who built them, but from the customers who participated.

You'll read stories from huge companies like HP and the Mini brand of BMW. You'll also hear from little guys like Blendtec, maker of a $399 blender that's been successfully promoted through YouTube, and eBags, the fast-growing online luggage site. In the business-to-business sector, you'll see successesful applications by accounting firm Ernst & Young, technology vendor Tibco, and email marketing services provider Constant Contact.

Marketers like you are creating these applications right now, in the midst of the economic downturn. If they can do it, so can you. And when you're done with this book, drop by our Web site at groundswell. forrester.com, where you'll see everything from award-winning groundswell applications to consumer data. I look forward to hearing about your successes.

Josh Bernoff, March 2009

# Listening to the Groundswell

Lynn Perry has cancer. In fact, he has had three forms of terminal cancer: prostate cancer, which spread to the bones; lung cancer; and cancer of the epiglottis. The treatments to his throat give him a hoarse, smoky voice like a country singer, which fits pretty well since he's a Harley-riding, keyboard-playing ex-engineer from Plano, Texas.

Perry (everybody calls him Perry) has an engineering background that makes him a pretty analytical guy, in his own down-home country philosopher way. He doesn't sound sad about his cancer—he's lived with it for six years and will keep going until he can't anymore. He's sixty-six, and he reserves his sympathy for people he feels are worse off than him—children he's met while waiting for treatment, for example. Although he doesn't waste too much time on emotional "cancer talk," as he puts it, he does have a fair amount to say about cancer treatment and the way it's delivered. With the analytical mind-set he brings to it, you listen and realize his perspective is well worth hearing.

"There are things that make me question M. D. Anderson," says Perry. (M. D. Anderson is the major cancer treatment center in Houston, where he goes for treatment.) "They give you this little document; they're very insistent on patient promptness. I am there right on the button. I sit there, wait an hour, an hour and a half, two hours. There is something wrong with this picture. My time is more precious than theirs." (At this point Perry reveals that if the doctors are right, he'll be dead in less than six months.) "Patients complain if the wait is too long, so they won't go to that [cancer treatment center]. I don't care if they have a faith healer in there, a mundane reason like the wait will stop 'em. 'I had to sit there for four hours,' they say, and they won't go again. The best hospitals and the best rankings [he means the published rankings from *U.S. News & World Report*] don't faze those type patients at all."

M. D. Anderson, Perry's cancer center, prides itself on its reputation. *U.S. News & World Report* ranks it tops in the nation. It just spent $125 million on a proton therapy cancer treatment center, the most advanced treatment technology there is. If a cancer can be treated, M. D. Anderson can treat it.

But that's all for naught if, as Lynn Perry points out, the patients give up and walk out.

As it turns out, though, M. D. Anderson has made listening to patients like Lynn Perry a priority. M. D. Anderson is investing major efforts in improving its scheduling. Why? Because it's put a priority on listening—and because it's figured out ways to integrate opinions like Lynn Perry's into its research, every bit as much as it pays attention to medical research. Which is a good thing since, according to Perry, those impatient patients may prefer to go to their local community hospital instead of M. D. Anderson—and it's going to need a lot of patients and a lot of treatments to pay for that proton therapy center.

## Your Brand Is What Your Customers Say It Is

Marketers tell us they define and manage brands. Some spend millions, or hundreds of millions, of dollars on advertising. They carefully extend brand names, putting Scope on a tube of toothpaste to see what happens. We bought this brand, they say. We spent on it. We own it.

Bull.

Your brand is whatever your customers say it is. And in the groundswell where they communicate with each other, they decide.

One of the most brilliant brand theorists we've ever met is Ricardo Guimarães, founder of Thymus

Branding, in São Paulo, Brazil. After running a big Brazilian ad agency for a long time, Guimarães started his consultancy to spread a new way of thinking. He says brands belong to customers, not companies. In his words:

> The value of a brand belongs to the market, and not to the company. The company in this sense is a tool to create value for the brand . . . Brand in this sense—it lives outside the company, not in the company. When I say that the management is not prepared for dealing with the brand, it is because in their mind-set they are managing a closed structure that is the company. The brand is an open structure—they don't know how to manage an open structure.

For example, M. D. Anderson thinks its brand is defined by a shiny new $125 million proton therapy center. But Lynn Perry thinks part of the M. D. Anderson brand is about making him wait. What do your customers think *your* brand is about?

There's one way to find out. You have to listen.

If you were in charge of marketing for M. D. Anderson, you'd probably like some way to put Lynn Perry and three hundred other cancer patients on call, ask them how they make treatment decisions, ask them what's on their minds. If you were smart, you would listen in as they talk to each other and learn how they think. This is *listening to the groundswell,* and it's exactly what several cancer centers around the United States (including M. D. Anderson) did. They hired a company called Communispace to recruit and manage a private community of cancer patients, and those patients are now revealing how they think, every day. That's current, continuous insight on demand, and it's the topic of this chapter.

## What Do We Mean by Listening?

Cynics will tell you that companies never listen to their customers. That's completely untrue. They not only listen to their customers; they pay large amounts of money to do so, very, very carefully. They just don't call it listening. They call it market research. Market research is very good at finding answers to questions. It's just not so effective at generating insights.

Companies pay over $15 billion annually for market research. For example, marketers paid Nielsen over $3.7 billion in 2006 for information about which products were selling in stores; what television programs people were watching; and what music, books, and Web sites people were consuming. In the same

5

year, health care companies paid over $2 billion to IMS Health, which reports information about what conditions doctors are diagnosing and which drugs are prescribed to whom. It's safe to say that Lynn Perry's complaints about scheduling were not included in those IMS Health reports.

Companies pay money for syndicated research sources like Nielsen and IMS Health because they all want answers to similar questions (for example, how many people are watching *Heroes*, or how well is Viagra selling?). Syndicated research is a valuable tool for mapping trends, but it can't tell you what people are thinking.

Marketers also pay handsomely for their own surveys. A mail, phone, or Internet survey of a thousand consumers will tell you what those thousand consumers are thinking about the questions you ask them. Those surveys typically cost at least $10,000 and, with expert analysis, can easily cost over $100,000, especially if the people you'd like to survey are hard to find, like people with cancer. Designed cleverly enough, these surveys will answer any question you can think up. But they can't tell you what you never thought to ask. And what you never thought to ask might be the most important question for your business.

Finally, there are focus groups. For $7,000 to $15,000, you can listen to ten or fifteen people for a couple of hours as they react to whatever you throw at them. Here, finally, you can get a spontaneous reaction, and you may hear something that surprises you—that is, if you get lucky and happen to get someone as thoughtful as Lynn Perry in your focus group.

Come to think of it, the most thoughtful people among your target customers don't want to take your surveys or be in your focus groups. The thoughtful people may not be on those survey panels, and they may not show up for your focus groups; even if they are, those research methods are designed to answer questions, not to tap into consumer insights.

### Listening to the Groundswell Reveals New Insights

If only there were some way to observe your customers in their natural habitats, as it were, you could get beyond the bias of surveys and the limitations of focus groups. Ideally, you could observe hundreds, if not thousands, of the people you'd like to know more about. You'd watch them as they interacted with your company, your competitors, and each other in the course of their normal day-to-day business. It would be even better if they'd take notes about their own behavior so that you'd have a record of what they were thinking.

Thanks to the groundswell, this kind of insight is available. Consumers in the groundswell are leaving clues about their opinions, positive and negative, on a daily or hourly basis. If you have a retail store, they're blogging about your store experience, your selection, and their favorite products. If you make TV sets, shoes, or tires—just about anything—they're on discussion forums dissecting the pros and cons of your product's features, your prices, and your customer support. They're rating your products and services on Yelp and TripAdvisor. And it's all there for you to listen to.

By itself, analyzing this activity has problems. To begin with, you won't hear from everybody; you'll only hear from people willing to talk. So listening to the groundswell comes with a huge caveat—you'll gain new insights, but don't assume that the people you hear from are representative.

Even so, the very volume of comments out there is a vast source of information. And that's the second problem. Volume. There's so much information flowing out of the groundswell, it's like watching a thousand television channels at once. To make sense of it, you need to apply some technology, boiling down the chatter to a manageable stream of insights.

As you might imagine, a bunch of technology companies have sprung up to solve these problems. In the rest of this chapter, we'll show you how to use their services to gain insights from the groundswell— groundswell thinking applied to research.

## Two Listening Strategies

There are lots of ways to listen to the groundswell. Google your product name along with the word *sucks* or *awesome,* for example. Do a blog search on Technorati. Or check out what the people who have tagged your company or your products on del.icio.us are saying. But in working with clients, we've seen that these homegrown monitoring methods don't scale. To gain real insight, you're better off working with vendors that provide professional tools. There are two basic ways to do this:

1. *Set up your own private community.* That's how cancer centers like M. D. Anderson were able to learn about the insights from Lynn Perry. A private community is like a continuously running, huge, engaged focus group—a natural interaction in a setting where you can listen in. One primary supplier of private communities is Communispace, although the category is growing rapidly with similar products from the vendors MarketTools and

Networked Insights. We'll describe how private communities work in the first case in this chapter.

2. *Begin brand monitoring.* Hire a company to listen to the Internet—blogs, discussion forums, YouTube, and everything else—on your behalf. Then have it deliver to you neat summary reports about what's happening or push the results out to departments, like customer service, that can address pressing customer issues. There are dozens of companies that will do this, starting with two that were acquired by a couple of the largest research companies on the planet: Nielsen's BuzzMetrics and TNS's Cymfony. We'll show the power of blog monitoring in the second case in this chapter, which looks at the car company Mini.

One more thing: listening by itself is sterile. Those neat reports that come from Communispace and BuzzMetrics are a waste of cash if they sit on the shelf. To profit from listening, you need a plan to *act* on what you learn. That's what you'll see in these cases from the National Comprehensive Cancer Network and Mini, and it's why their listening strategies paid off.

## Case Study

## National Comprehensive Cancer Network: Listening with a Private Community

Ellen Sonet, VP of marketing for New York's Memorial Sloan-Kettering Cancer Center, is passionate about customers' insights. "To me as a marketing person, it's most important that I understand what it feels like to be my consumer," she told us.

Now, anybody can say that, but based on what Ellen told us about her background, we believe her.

Earlier in her career, when she was marketing over-the-counter pharmaceutical products, she would hang out in drugstores and observe customers. "Why did he pick up that other nasal spray and not mine?" she would think. Hours and hours of this sort of observation went into plans for everything from advertising to packaging.

In the past ten years, as the top marketer at Memorial Sloan-Kettering, she's had to develop new methods. As you might imagine, marketers aren't powerful in the hospital world—doctors are. Doctors interact with patients. Doctors know best. Doctors are in charge. Memorial Sloan-Kettering has nine thousand employees. Counting Ellen, three and a half of those work in marketing.

Ellen regularly volunteers to deliver flowers to patients, just to get a feel for what's going on with her customers. But there's only so much to be learned from that, since she can't really interact with the patients in any meaningful way. Which is why, when Ellen Sonet met Diane Hessan at a marketing event in 2003, she became certain they needed to work together.

Diane Hessan is the CEO of Communispace, one of the most rapidly growing vendors in the groundswell. Communispace has set up hundreds of private communities for its clients, which include over seventy-five companies, ranging from hair care and breakfast cereal to financial services and IT advice. Communispace's service is relatively simple to describe. The company recruits three hundred to five hundred people in the client's target market—young men for Axe body spray, or people trying to lose weight for GlaxoSmithKline's alli weight control drug. Those recruits form a community that looks like any other online social network, with profiles, discussion forums, online chat, and uploaded photos. But this network is a *research* network. No one can see it except the members, the moderators from Communispace, and the client.

A Communispace community is a listening machine that generates insight. It's a miniature groundswell in a box. The members typically are thanked with inexpensive Amazon gift certificates. They look just like groundswell participants out in the real world, except that they promise to spend an hour a week on the site. Communispace has duplicated the features that make other communities so interactive, and as a result, the participants behave in a very natural way—not at all like the stilted one-time interactions in a focus group, for example.

Of course, there was the little problem of money—a Communispace community costs at least $180,000 for a six-month trial and about $20,000 per month after that, and Ellen had very little budget. But Memorial Sloan-Kettering is part of the National Comprehensive Cancer Network (NCCN), a group of twenty-one dedicated cancer centers around the country. All the NCCN centers had a similar need to learn about their patients. It took two years, but Ellen convinced several of the NCCN cancer centers to go in with her on a Communispace community. Both Communispace and the cancer centers invited cancer patients to join the community and recruited over three hundred of them. Then Ellen began listening.

### Research Information Versus Community Insights

Research goes where you expect it to go. You find out whether people will spend an extra $100 if the TV is six inches bigger. You see whether Hispanics really respond to your new TV commercial.

Ellen Sonet started with this same approach, but right away she got a surprise. The first question the NCCN members asked the community was the most important: how did you decide where to get treated?

The prevailing wisdom among the doctors at Memorial Sloan-Kettering was that patients choose their treatment center based on reputation. Since patients want the best chance for a successful outcome, they would choose to go to a world-renowned cancer center like Memorial Sloan-Kettering. So the most important thing was to make sure the public recognized the cancer center's outstanding expertise.

Wrong.

A cancer patient does not make decisions like a business executive choosing what supplier to work with. Imagine it. You've just been diagnosed with cancer. It's shocking and terrifying, and you're ignorant. You're meeting new doctors for the first time, and now you have a crucial decision to make: where to go for treatment.

Want to know how this feels? Here's a comment from "Tracy D" in the Communispace forum:[1]

As I'm sure you know, when you hear a diagnosis of cancer, you go into a tailspin. You are coping with so many fears and emotions, yet you want to know as much as you can. The Web has been invaluable for that, but I really appreciated [my doctor] taking charge and telling me where he thought I should go. There was really no discussion about it. I was not capable of discussion at the time.

Like Tracy, more than half of patients cite *their primary care physician* as important in the recommendation on where to get treatment. The primary care physician is typically a trusted professional the patient has been seeing for years. So in the stressful days after a cancer diagnosis, many a patient falls back on the familiar, regardless of the lofty reputation a cancer center may have made for itself.

Already the community had proved its worth. Memorial Sloan-Kettering still prides itself on its outstanding reputation among consumers and uses marketing to maintain that image. But Ellen Sonet now had the proof she needed to change the way a 9,000-employee cancer center markets itself. "We have not historically had the best relationships with community docs, yet they are an important source of referrals for us," she said. So she began to change things. "I . . . instituted many programs to improve our relationships with community [primary care physicians], urologists, and ob-gyns," she points out. Change had begun.

People who fill out surveys don't really care what happens next. Cancer patients in an ongoing community do. Seven out of ten visit the community every week. And it's not the gift certificates that drive them—two out of three community members said they received greater value from the community itself. Here's a typical comment: "If there is ANYTHING I have learned it is that the more connections we make with folks with the same kind of cancer the better the information we can learn about how to deal with it." Research is one-way. A community, even a research community like this one, offers a more lasting value. Of seventy-six discussions in the NCCN community, only eighteen were initiated by the moderators—the rest were started by the members themselves.

We mentioned that listening does no good unless you act on it. Here's a perfect example. NCCN asked cancer patients, "Where do you get information about your diagnosis and treatment?" Out of 81 respondents, 78 looked for information on the Internet. Out of 114 respondents, 106 said they were likely to recommend the Internet as a source of information. These results were overwhelmingly clear, but any survey could have revealed them (although getting cancer patients into a survey would be challenging). In fact, given that these respondents were already members of an Internet community, there is clearly some online bias present here.

But the community allowed people to converse and tell *what* they looked for and *how* they used it in ways that no survey could. Here, in part, is what Lynn Perry, the Harley-riding engineer we met at the start of the chapter, said about how he uses online resources:

(2) What sources of information did/do you use to learn about treatment options?

I spent hours and hours on the Internet, looking for info I was totally unfamiliar [with] at the time. I was on numerous sites that included [the American Cancer Society], NCCN, [the National Cancer Institute], and a dozen or so sites of the top U.S. Clinics. Although much information I found on one site would be redundantly duplicated on another, it was all helpful. As I recall, the ACS site was the most helpful because it had numerous resource links as well as a diagnostic tool . . . I also downloaded M.D. Anderson's treatment guidelines . . .

(3) Where did you/do you go to find out about long-term effects of your treatment, side-effects of treatment, etc.?

(a) Although much of this type [of] info was also found in sites described in (2), above, I relied more heavily on info I downloaded from the drug or chemo manufacturers' website whose product I was researching. I also used info published on professional oncology sites, oncology journals, and European oncology sites.

(4) Throughout this process, which sources have been especially helpful? Which have not? Who are they?

(a) . . . Those that have been especially helpful include the ACS, NCCN, NCI, the "search" feature on M.D. Anderson's website, and M.D. Anderson's downloadable PDF files of their guidelines.

No survey could get to this—Lynn Perry's personal guide to cancer resources on the Internet. Groundswell thinking applied to research had yielded a far more detailed set of insights.

Many doctors hate the Internet because it lets patients get their own information, some of which is of dubious quality. (One patient reported that when she brought up information she found online, her doctor responded, "Stay off the Internet!") But it's now abundantly clear to doctors at NCCN cancer centers that they must have an Internet strategy, and the Communispace community is helping them figure it out.

Ellen Sonet is helping build Web resources for her cancer center right now. She knows that patients go to cancer organizations like the American Cancer Society more, WebMD a little less, and cancer center Web sites even less than that. She even knows (since Communispace asked) which search terms people use—you could guess that it makes sense for her to buy "breast cancer" keywords on Google, but would you have guessed that lots of people search on "metastatic"? From this, she can populate Memorial Sloan-Kettering's site with information and make it both a jumping-off point and a search destination for cancer patients. And that will improve patients' affinity for her cancer center.

## The Real Power of Listening

Ellen Sonet started from a position of weakness, a marketer in a doctor's world. Now she has insights. This has a side effect. It's called respect.

"What started as a marketing project has a quasi-clinical halo," she told us. She presented a poster session of her research findings at a medical meeting, a role nearly always filled before this by clinicians and medical researchers.

Because she's tapped into Communispace's private cancer community, Ellen has become a part of more decisions at her organization. She described how a nurse was looking to do research on compliance with oral chemotherapy: "She was talking about doing focus groups. By the time you get them budgeted, set up, and recruited . . . it could take six months. Or we could turn it around in two weeks and spend nothing incremental [that is, no additional cost in surveying the Communispace community]." Own the resource that generates the insights, and you have clout.

This change isn't unusual; it's typical. For example, at Unilever, Alison Zelen is in charge of consumer and market insights for deodorants in North America. She set up a private community to study young guys, the target market for Axe bodyspray. Like Ellen Sonet, Alison is keen to know everything about her customers—to get inside their heads. She had the young men in her community upload pictures of their rooms, use the language that comes naturally, and talk about their attitudes about everything from music to girls. Girls, as you might expect, are central. And the result of Alison's research is that Axe was positioned dead-on as attracting the opposite sex, with ads that spoke to young men in the terminology and settings they find familiar. Alison had acted on her insights. Those ads rang true because she knows an awful lot about how young men think.

The other effect, as with Ellen Sonet, is that Alison Zelen's profile has risen. She got quoted in publications ranging from the *Boston Globe* to *Advertising Age,* which published an interview with her titled "For Axe Star, It Sure Helps to Think Like Guy." It pays to have your own community on call for insights.

The popularity of private communities has spread because they deliver not just insights but actionable insights. Charles Schwab used private communities to get inside the heads of Generation X investors, discovered that these consumers start their investment thinking at their checking accounts, and then launched a high-yield checking account and redesigned its site. Payoff: 32 percent more Generation X investors over the previous year. Network Solutions, which sells domain names and Web design solutions to small businesses, built a small-business owners community and learned that the language in its marketing pages didn't match the way that these business owners talk. It also made its Web design tool far more flexible and easy to use by implementing changes it piloted with the private community. Payoff: a 10 percent increase in some attributes of customer satisfaction, an important measure for a service that charges tight-fisted business owners by the month.

As we've shown, having your own community has significant advantages—you can ask members whatever you want. But that's only one way to listen to the groundswell. Another is just to put your ear to the ground and see what people everywhere are talking about. That's brand monitoring, and it's the subject of our next case.

## Case Study

## Mini USA: Listening Through Brand Monitoring

Trudy Hardy faced an interesting challenge in 2006. As head of marketing for Mini USA, the American arm of BMW's Mini Cooper brand, she had to keep her cute little car relevant. Competitors like Volkswagen and Honda were releasing new models in the small-car segment. In the car business, everything revolves around new models—they generate press, which generates buzz, which generates sales. Mini had . . . well, the same cars it had the previous year. Mini had grown significantly since Trudy launched the brand five years earlier, but how could she keep it on a growth path?

As the brand's steward since its inception, Trudy had confidence in the cars. She knew Mini owners loved their vehicles. But what did they love, and how could Mini take advantage of that? To understand and answer this question, Mini decided to monitor online chatter about its cars—to listen in on the natural conversation. This had two benefits. First, it helped reveal how Mini owners felt. And second, it enabled Mini to measure the effects of its own marketing efforts by monitoring buzz before and after.

## Monitoring Spawns a Radical Idea—Marketing to Existing Customers

First of all, are enough Mini owners likely to be interacting online to make the buzz worth monitoring? Our research at Forrester shows that people with Mini cars and other competing brands like Honda and Volkswagen are indeed active participants in social activities, both creating content and reacting to content created by others, so it's well worth listening to what they have to say.

Mini and its agency—Butler, Shine, Stern & Partners—selected MotiveQuest to monitor the brand's online buzz. MotiveQuest is one of half a dozen companies, including Nielsen's BuzzMetrics and TNS's Cymfony, that offer brand-monitoring services. All these companies have moved to automatic monitoring, not just of blogs, but of the entire online chatter associated with a brand: discussion groups, forums, MySpace pages, and so on. Some cost more, some cost less; MotiveQuest is among the most expensive, typically charging $70,000 per project. While its competitors also track positive and negative sentiment in thousands of online comments and blog posts, MotiveQuest goes further, tracking responses by analyzing five hundred expressions of emotional sentiment with names like "inspiration," "anger," "hatred," "relaxation," and "excitement," developed in conjunction with the marketing whizzes at Northwestern University's Kellogg School of Management.

At the start of MotiveQuest's analysis in mid-2006, the Mini brand was generating more online discussion than any of the competing brands MotiveQuest was tracking, with the exception of the Volkswagen Jetta. And the Mini comments were four times more likely to be positive than negative. But MotiveQuest and Mini had to look deeper to see what was really going on. Mini owners scored well above average on community activities, like sharing pictures and joining local clubs. Here's a typical comment:[2]

I have never been involved in another car culture. Friends who are tell me when they meet MINI owners that our culture is in some ways very familiar—complete obsession with the MINIs—and in some ways very different—it seems to transcend the car. We get to know each other on a much more personal level.

So where Camaro owners might talk about their car's power and Lexus owners about their car's luxurious styling, Mini owners would rather see themselves as members of an exclusive club of people who belonged together. As the first buyers of this odd little car, they bonded with each other. They identified themselves—and each other—*as* Mini owners.

Here, then, was the key to making sure Mini was not another Chrysler PT Cruiser or Volkswagen Beetle—a car that's fashionable for a few years and then falls out of favor. Mini USA needed to strengthen the community, which would itself go out and proselytize others to the brand. According to J.D. Power and Associates, in 2006 Mini outranked every other brand in owners' likelihood to recommend the car to others.

This insight led Trudy and her agency to a radical conclusion: it was time to market to Mini *owners*, not prospective Mini *buyers*. Think of that. Every car company in the world spends its marketing dollars trying to convince people to buy a new car. Once you've bought, you generate cost, not revenue, as you consume warranty service. And Mini now proposed to spend its money on people who've already bought the car? That took guts. But marketing to your own owners in hopes of spreading word of mouth—that's groundswell thinking.

At Mini, Trudy Hardy said, "I had the ability to be brave and try new things . . . At Jaguar [her previous company], it was difficult to be brave, I couldn't get people to try new things, let alone buy into a brave approach." The result was a completely radical ad campaign that mystified the advertising community even as it captivated the Mini owners. Mini sent owners a decoder package and then created ads with coded messages that only they could read. The company created "Mini Takes the States," a series of rallies for Mini owners all across America. And it worked, at least from the buzz perspective. In a year in which Mini sold thirty-eight thousand cars, over three thousand owners came to Mini events, spawning over twenty-one hundred photos posted on Flickr and eight YouTube videos. Here's what one owner said about the secret decoder:

> lol [laughing out loud] I like that. It just takes some brains to figure it out! Most MINI owners are pretty smart, so . . . lol Nice find. Thanks for sharing!

Buzz measurement by MotiveQuest revealed that the idea of targeting existing owners was working—they were talking. But did this translate into sales?

## *The Relationship Between Buzz and Sales*

There's no proof—yet—that online buzz leads directly to sales in every industry. But vendors like Motive-Quest and academics are finding more and more evidence that with the right measurements, online word of mouth is a leading indicator for sales.

From working with mobile phone makers, Motive-Quest CEO David Rabjohns had already seen evidence that an increase in positive comments about a handset typically appeared a month or two before an increase in market share for that handset. MotiveQuest began working with a team at Northwestern University, including marketing professor Jacquelyn Thomas, on metrics that could nail down this correlation across multiple industries.

Analyzing monthly sales data for Mini, David saw the same pattern. MotiveQuest and Northwestern created an indicator they called the "online promoter score"—an estimate of the online chatter likely to lead to a recommendation. For seven months between February and August 2006, the pattern was clear—when the online promoter activity went up, sales went up in the following month. When the activity went down, sales went down.

After August the dynamic changed, in part because Mini's word of mouth began spiking as a result of its earlier marketing focused on the customer community. At the same time word leaked out that a new Mini model was coming, which can depress current-month sales as people wait for the new car. But overall Mini's sales in 2006 were down only 4 percent from 2005, a decline that Trudy attributes to production constraints. In a year with no new models, this is excellent performance. Mini had saved 2006, in part because of marketing to its own customers and listening as the groundswell responded.

## Listening to the Groundswell: What It Means to You

Listening is perhaps the most essential neglected skill in business. Part of the reason is that it's always been so hard. The result was the narrowest form of listening—market research. But in the era of the groundswell, listening is easy. Not listening, on the other hand, is criminal.

Whether you choose to start a private community, engage a company for brand monitoring, or just use the available tools to do rudimentary listening on your own, your organization must get started. Here are six reasons why:

1. *Find out what your brand stands for.* You know the message you're trying to get across. How

is that different from what people are talking about? Mini thought its brand was about a snappy, cool way to deliver an experience they called *motoring*. The company was right, but needed brand monitoring to realize its brand was also about a community. If Brazilian brand theorist Ricardo Guimarães is right, then your brand is whatever people say it is. You'd better find out what they're saying. This applies not just to traditional media but to how you talk to the groundswell—a topic we cover in detail in the next chapter.

2. *Understand how buzz is shifting.* Start listening, and you have a baseline. Keep listening, and you understand change. Is your competitor getting all the talk? Are people talking less about your style and more about your high prices? Surveys can find this out at a coarse degree of resolution. Listening to the groundswell gives you the answer in high definition, on a weekly or even daily basis. And as more evidence accumulates that buzz is a leading indicator for sales, you'd better be paying attention. This tracking also enables you to find people with problems and connect with them to address their problems

directly. In fact, Dell is using this technique with Visible Technologies to head off support issues with squeaky wheels on blogs and forums.

3. *Save research money; increase research responsiveness.* If you do a survey once in a while, listening is more expensive. But if your company has a regular research budget, some of it should go to listening. A private community like the ones offered by Communispace, once it's up and running, can deliver survey results far more quickly than a custom survey. And it allows you to ask "why," which ordinary surveys don't do so well. Brand monitoring is no substitute for traditional research, but it can fill in the details once you've identified a trend.

4. *Find the sources of influence in your market.* Who's talking about your product? Are the bloggers more influential, or are the discussion forums? Are thousands of people watching videos about it on YouTube? Has somebody scooped up your identity on MySpace or started a community around it on Facebook? Monitoring vendors like BuzzLogic specialize in identifying who

has influence. Once you find the influencers, you can cultivate them.

5. *Manage PR crises.* If your company is going to suffer an assault from the groundswell— a negative YouTube video, a rapidly spreading blog post, bad buzz on forums— you'll hear about it earlier if you're listening. Brand monitoring can function as an early-warning system, allowing your organization to respond before things get out of hand. In these situations, hours can count.

6. *Generate new product and marketing ideas.* Your customers use your products and services all the time. They generate lots of intelligent ideas about those products and services, and they will offer those ideas to you—*for free*. Is there a Lynn Perry in your market, describing how your service should be made more efficient? Is there a blogger suggesting new features or packaging for your products? Maybe a discussion group has figured out what your new marketing message should be or a new type of store you should sell through. You can get access to all these ideas, but only if you listen.

## Your Listening Plan

So if you've decided to start listening, what should you do? From our experience working with companies, listening generally starts in the research or marketing department. Over time, though, listening will become a responsibility that is spread throughout an organization (we show some examples of this in chapter 10). Here are some practical suggestions that will help you succeed with listening to the groundswell:

- *Check how active your customers are with social technologies.* Listening is most effective if your customers are *in* the groundswell to begin with. Check, in particular, the number of people who create content in your customer base. If those numbers are high—at least 15 percent of your customers—then you can use brand monitoring effectively to listen to your market (this applies to most car brands, for example). If they're very high—30 percent or more—then brand monitoring becomes an imperative (as with most technology products and services). Less than 15 percent means you'll be listening to a narrower slice of your audience, which may still be worthwhile but won't be remotely representative (this will happen if your audience skews older, for example). In that case, you may want to consider a private community instead.

- *Start small, think big.* For large companies with many brands, undertaking an overall brand-monitoring program can escalate into the million-dollar price range rapidly. Instead, start with a single brand and monitor that. Private communities also work best on a single brand or customer segment, like Alison Zelen's young men for Unilever's deodorant brands. But over and over again, we've seen these programs spread, based on their utility to the company. Imagine for a moment that your listening program spreads to five or ten times the cost and complexity you start with. Who will manage that, and how? Can your vendors grow with you? It's best to think these questions through before you begin so you'll be prepared.

- *Make sure your listening vendor has dedicated an experienced team to your effort.* Monitoring and community companies are new enough that it's likely to be the CEO, head of marketing, or head of sales who pitches you. They're smart. Are their staffs as well? "You need to focus specifically on the team you will be getting, the analysts at the vendor," says analyst Peter Kim, Forrester's expert on brand monitoring. Since this is a new world you'll be navigating, you'll want an experienced team to help you create and manage the information coming in and to understand the results.

- *Choose a senior person to interpret the information and integrate it with other sources.* Paying hundreds of thousands of dollars for a community or monitoring service and failing to exploit the information is like buying a private jet and forgetting where you parked it. Listening generates insights, but they won't sneak up and shout in your ears—you need to manage this resource. One staffer needs to dedicate time to reading the reports, interfacing with the vendors, and suggesting new information to retrieve. This staffer should be able to integrate the insights from listening to the groundswell with other syndicated research, surveys, and focus groups to create a complete market picture. If this is your job, be prepared—you'll be interfacing with marketing, product development, and other brands before long, which should boost your status, as it did for Ellen Sonet at Memorial Sloan-Kettering.

## How Listening Will Change Your Organization

So even as you get smarter by listening to the groundswell, you should prepare for some of the ways it will change your organization. Once you begin to listen and act on that information, your company will never be the same.

First, it's likely to change the power structure of your organization. Market research departments tend to be sequestered off to the side, a resource used by marketers and development teams. Whatever department takes charge of listening to the groundswell—whether it's research or marketing—will soon become far more central to how decisions are made. As happened with Ellen Sonet at Memorial Sloan-Kettering, expect marketing and research to exert a more powerful influence on development. Of course, this can lead to conflict with powerful development groups. That's why it's so important to package up the results of listening in ways that other groups in your organization can understand. Your job becomes to communicate what you've learned—to turn insight into change.

Second, the instant availability of information from customers can become like a drug that companies can become addicted to. Organizations that are used to

near-real-time feedback (like ratings in the TV industry and point-of-sale data in retail) have learned to bal-
ance the short-term scorekeeping with the long-term
strategy. But unlike simple scorekeeping, listening to
the groundswell is richer and applies to far more
industries. As listening becomes a bigger part of your
company, you should integrate the results into corporate decision making. For example, at a retailer, the
executive in charge of listening should become a regular part of buying and merchandising decisions; in a
brand company, she should become a regular fixture in
advertising strategy meetings.

Third is what we call the no-more-being-stupid
factor. Every company has stupid products, policies,
and organizational quirks. These corporate elements
persist because a top executive is biased toward them,
or because they're baked into corporate processes
and systems, or just because of tradition. Maybe
every transaction gets a legal review that delays it a
day but hasn't revealed a problem in the past two
years. Maybe your promises that the service techni-
cian will show up during a particular four-hour win-
dow are right only 75 percent of the time. Listening
to the groundswell will relentlessly reveal your stu-
pidity. When customers can complain, bitterly and
accurately, about the way you do business and you
can *measure and quantify* their complaints, it's hard to

deny your own flaws. The constituency for stupid policies and products will evaporate in the face of highly visible customer feedback.

Finally, you may think that listening is the easiest way to engage with the groundswell because it's low risk—it doesn't require you to put yourself into the conversation. But while listening is part of a conversation, every conversation includes talking as well. Listening to the groundswell and then speaking through traditional media and advertising is like responding to a friend's whispered confidence with a bullhorn. Listeners inevitably feel the temptation to respond by talking *within* the groundswell, by publishing blogs, contributing to user-generated content sites, and setting up communities. So if you're listening now, expect to be talking soon, too.

Talking—the other side of the conversation—is the topic of the next chapter. In it we describe a variety of techniques for entering the groundswell as a speaker, not just a listener.

# Talking with the Groundswell

Steve Ogborn is a management consultant with three teenage kids in a suburb of Chicago. One day in the summer of 2007, he was reading one of his favorite blogs—Engadget, which is aimed at lovers of personal technology—when he saw the unthinkable.

Some nut had put an Apple iPhone—the hottest technology product out there, just released—into a blender. The online video on Engadget featured a geeky-looking guy in a lab coat and safety goggles. The iPhone, in a matter of less than a minute, was reduced to dust (or "iSmoke" as the geeky-looking guy put it).

After this, Steve did two things.

First, he went to the Web site mentioned in the video—willitblend.com—and watched videos of the same blender destroying hockey pucks, cubic zirconia, and similar objects rarely seen in the average kitchen.

And second, somewhere in the back of his mind, an idea formed. Steve Ogborn's children love smoothies. "They eat their weight in fruit," he told us. His current blender just wasn't cutting it. So he checked out the blender in the videos, which was described in detail on willitblend.com.

The blender that had reduced the iPhone to dust cost $399. "My first reaction was 'boy, that's a lot for that blender,'" says Steve. But his extensive online investigation showed that Blendtec's $399 blender wasn't available anywhere else, either at that price or lower. So, thinking of his fruit-loving teenagers, he placed the order for the most expensive blender he'd ever owned.

It turns out, there are a lot of people like Steve Ogborn. Sales at Blendtec are up 20 percent since Blendtec's "Will It Blend?" series started appearing on sites like YouTube. Who's the genius who conceived this marketing program?

George Wright, marketing director for Blendtec, was an unlikely hero for the groundswell, having had no background in consumer marketing (or video) before joining Blendtec.

He conceived the idea of marketing with YouTube the day after he noticed sawdust all over the floor of the testing room—his techs had been grinding up two-by-two lumber as a way to test their heavy-duty blenders. Incredible, thought George. People have got to see this. And with that, he conceived the idea of putting extreme blending videos on the Internet. The first five videos cost a total of $50 to create. But with a little boost—Blendtec's Web expert, Ray Hansen, posted a link on Digg after setting up the videos on Blendtec's site—the videos caught fire, scoring 6 million views in the first week. (When George Wright told the CEO, Tom Dickson—the geeky-looking guy who starred in the videos—that he was now a hit on YouTube, his response was "WhoTube?" Tom knew the videos were going up on Blendtec's own site, but he had no idea that the video-sharing site even existed.) This was rapidly followed with appearances on VH1 and *The Today Show*. Later Jay Leno featured Tom Dickson on *The Tonight Show* (after blending a rake handle to splinters, Jay remarked, "[If] you need to get some fiber in your diet, this is perfect"). Soon people had viewed Blendtec's videos a total of 60 million times.

George Wright and Blendtec had created a consumer brand, basically, from a video camera and a few dollars' worth of goodies (true, destroying the iPod must have cost a few bucks, but nowhere near what it typically costs to film and place a TV commercial). Blendtec had exploited the groundswell's viral potential for marketing messages. George had cracked the code, in his own unique way, for talking with the groundswell.

## How Talking with the Groundswell Differs from Marketing

Companies already spend a lot of effort speaking to customers. This is the job of the marketing department. Two of the main—and expensive—methods they use are advertising and public relations.

Worldwide, marketers spent more than $400 billion on advertising in 2006, according to Pricewaterhouse-Coopers. Much of this money is spent on television commercials. This is not talking, this is *shouting*. Advertising thrives on repetition. The two main measures are reach (the gross number of individuals screamed at) and frequency (the number of times each one hears the shout). Advertising is about mass. "Advertise on the football game to reach more men" is as personal as it usually gets.

Public relations aims at exposures in free media. PR firms (still!) broadcast press releases about their clients' every deal and accomplishment—that McDonald's is trying to reduce trans fats, or that sales were up 3 percent at Toyota—to every reporter and "influencer" who might conceivably want to write about such stories. They hope these facts will get mentioned in the *Wall Street Journal* or featured on CNN or in a trade magazine.

Something's broken here, and you can see what it is in figure 2. It's the marketing funnel, a venerable metaphor that describes how consumers march down the path from awareness to purchase and loyalty. Shouting—advertising—herds them in the big end. Activities in the middle try to pull them down to that purchase, and if you're lucky, they come out the other end as customers.

With so many products trying to get people's attention, shouting at them isn't nearly as effective as it used to be. And once they reach the middle of the funnel, shouting hardly works at all. In analyzing this in a 2007 report, Forrester marketing analyst Brian Haven put it this way: "The funnel has outlived its usefulness as a metaphor. Face it: marketers no longer dictate the path people take, nor do they lead the dialogue." Once people are aware of your product, a new dynamic kicks in: people learning from *each other*. Social technologies have revved up that word-of-mouth dynamic, increasing the influence of regular people while diluting the value of traditional marketing. When we surveyed online consumers at the end of 2006, 83 percent said they trusted recommendations from friends and acquaintances, and more than half trusted online reviews from strangers. At the same time, trust in ads continued to plummet.

FIGURE 2

## The marketing funnel

*In traditional marketing theory, consumers are driven into the big end through awareness activities like advertising. They proceed through stages—including consideration, preference, and action—to become buyers. Marketers have little control over what happens in the middle stages, but the influence of the groundswell is heaviest there.*

Eyeballs →    Awareness   Consideration   Preference   Action   Loyalty   → Buyers

Customers in the middle of the funnel are engaged in conversations on blogs, in discussion forums, and in social networks. Your company can participate in these places, but shouting doesn't work. Conversations do. If your company creates a presence on a social network like Facebook, people will post comments and expect you to respond. If you put up a blog, they will comment and expect you to pay attention to those comments. These conversations require work, but they do influence people in the middle of the funnel—and not just those who comment, but those who read those comments, even if those readers never comment themselves.

Blendtec understands this. On the "Will It Blog" area of willitblend.com, George Wright tells you when and where you can see a blender demonstration in your town, and he invites visitors to suggest new things to blend. (That's how he got the idea to pulverize an iPod.) George Wright isn't just shouting; he's talking *with* his customers and listening as they talk back to him.

## Techniques for Talking with the Groundswell

There are lots of ways to talk with the groundswell. But for simplicity, we've narrowed them down to the ones that are the most common and most effective.

Here are the four that we will explore in more detail in this chapter:

1. *Post a viral video.* Put a video online, and let people share it. That's what Blendtec did with its extreme blending videos.

2. *Engage in social networks and user-generated content sites.* Creating a personality within social networking sites like MySpace is one of the simplest ways to extend your brand reach. Turning it into a conversation is harder.

3. *Join the blogosphere.* Empower your executives or staff to write blogs. Integral to this strategy is listening to and responding to other blogs in the blogosphere—and that's one way talking with blogs is different from issuing press releases. In this chapter we show how HP uses blogs to its advantage.

4. *Create a community.* Communities are a powerful way to engage with your customers and deliver value to them. They're also effective at delivering marketing messages, as long as you listen, not just shout. We'll show this through the example of Procter & Gamble's being-girl.com, a site for adolescent girls.

## Turning Viral Videos into a Conversation

For George Wright and Blendtec, "Will It Blend?" started out to be about awareness. It was, basically, a substitute for an advertising campaign. It was focused at the big end of the funnel.

Solving awareness problems with viral videos doesn't just work for consumer products—it can work in a business-to-business setting, too. Consider "Greg the Architect," an extremely cheesy video series from Tibco about service-oriented architecture (SOA) solutions—a service that appeals to information technology professionals who integrate applications. The "Greg the Architect" videos on YouTube follow the trials of a young and heroic software architect (played by an action figure) as he tries to make sense of technology strategy, dealing with his company's CIO and acronym-slinging technology vendors (played, of course, by other action figures, including Barbie, who makes a cameo). This is funny stuff, but it's for an extremely narrow audience—the series has racked up sixty thousand views on YouTube, far fewer than "Will It Blend?"

But as Tibco's head of worldwide direct marketing, Dan Ziman, explained to us, he's not trying to reach everybody—he's just trying to start a dialogue with big IT buyers. The typical Tibco SOA deal generates over $500,000 and may take six months or more to negotiate. So instead of pursuing sales, like Blendtec's George Wright, he's pursuing relationships. Since "Greg the Architect" started running, subscriptions to Tibco's SOA newsletter are up four-fold, which promotes the relationships the company needs. Faced with an awareness problem and well-funded competitors like IBM and Oracle, Dan found a cheap way to elbow his way in front of customers by treating them as people—people with needs that his videos portray in an empathetic, if satirical, way.

If you pursue this strategy, keep your objective in mind. Videos like Dan's and George's can get people's attention. What will you do once you have that attention?

Blendtec maintains, at willitblend.com, a site that makes it easy to learn more about the blenders and possibly order one. Tibco's videos create relationships through its newsletter. If your YouTube video doesn't create at least the beginning of a relationship, it's just another way of shouting.

To be most effective, these videos must allow people to interact. They should direct people to a social network, a blog, or a community where they can form further relationships with each other or with the company. These are the mechanisms that can help people in the middle of the funnel, and we discuss them in the rest of this chapter.

## Case Study

## Ernst & Young: Talking in Social Networks

Social networks are popular. For example, 25 percent of online adults in North America, 21 percent of Europeans, and 35 percent of South Koreans have joined them. Your customers are there. Where are you?

For example, consider Ernst & Young's problem. To keep up with its clients' needs, the global accounting firm has to hire thirty-five hundred new college grads every year. And since 74 percent of college students are members of social networks,[1] Ernst & Young (E&Y) meets them there, where they live. As Dan Black, director of campus recruiting for the Americas, told us, "Facebook stood out to us—at the time [we started], they told us that 85 percent of all college students have a profile."

On the day in 2007 that we looked, E&Y's careers group on Facebook had 8,469 members, of which 68 had joined that day. What sets E&Y apart, though, is the dialogue it creates within the site. Dan demonstrates real groundswell thinking by realizing that it's student-to-student communication that sets this medium apart. "This generation puts a lot of stock in the opinion and advice and direction of their peers," he says, an argument he used to justify the Facebook effort to the firm's executive management. And while he's extremely busy with all that hiring, he still makes time to answer questions posted on the "wall" for Ernst & Young's Facebook page because he knows his target students are reading the results. Here's a typical dialogue:

DJ: Hello, I am completing my MBA . . . next summer double majoring in Accounting and Finance from UMass Boston. What do you suggest to apply for an internship or fulltime entry level positions ? . . . Thank you, DJ

Dan: . . . Please send a message via Facebook directly to Julia DeWolfe . . . [S]he is our Boston recruiter and will be best able to assess your candidacy.

DJ: Thanks Dan. I have one more question. Do you consider [a] candidate for only that particular location he has applied or [do] you consider [an] application for openings nationwide?

Dan: To answer your question, we interview each candidate once during the process. If you do well, you certainly have the option to discuss different locations. However, if you do not do well in the interview we do not permit you to interview with someone else in another location. This is because our interview model is such that the first interview will cover the same information regardless of who is doing the interviewing from EY.

Let's tie this back to the funnel. Through advertising on campus and on Facebook, Ernst & Young makes its target audience—college students—aware of the company. E&Y's career's page on Facebook is also filled with information, videos, and other traditional advertising elements. But *beyond* awareness, E&Y uses Facebook to draw students into the process further at their own pace and answers questions individually. E&Y is talking *with* these candidates, rather than just shouting at them. And while you might think this is a lot of trouble for each candidate, remember that others visiting E&Y's page can see this dialogue. Any of the college students who has "friended" Ernst & Young's careers page—made friends with it, as they would a person—can get notices of these updates. Students can also interact with each other there. For a decision as big as where to take that first job, this type of connection is powerful. And since an Ernst & Young staffer could easily generate millions of dollars in audit, tax, or similar services over the course of her career, the efforts on this site are well worth it.

*Ways to Use—and Measure—The Results
of Participation in Social Networks*

The key to succeeding in social networks is to help people spread your message and to measure the result.

To understand how these efforts work, consider what Adidas and its agencies, Isobar and Carat, did with its soccer shoes. Visitors to www.myspace.com/adidassoccer are invited to choose between two philosophies of soccer and two types of shoes; they choose the Predator if their approach is team oriented and precise or F50 Tunit if they're more about showmanship. Adidas knows its audience and their passions—of more than fifty thousand MySpace members who made friends with Adidas soccer, the split between Predator and F50 Tunit was nearly even. The site is filled with opportunities to taunt the other side and to change your own MySpace profile with wallpaper and graphics from Adidas—interactions that go way beyond shouting by engaging visitors.

Engagement pays off. According to Market Evolution—a consultancy that analyzed the campaign for MySpace and Carat in a 2007 report called "Never Ending Friending"[2]—every $100,000 spent in advertising drove twenty-six thousand people to become more likely to buy, based on their exposure to Adidas's

MySpace page. But beyond that, many of those passed along the brand to their friends, resulting in thousands of more pages featuring Adidas soccer graphics and eighteen thousand additional people whose likelihood to buy had increased. And beyond *that*, over 4 million people were exposed to the brand on those members' pages. This is the effect that makes talking through social networks so powerful.

Even more compelling are examples from South Korea, where the Cyworld social network dominates. Pizza Hut launched a new Italian-style pizza with an ad campaign driving people to its "mini-hompy" (mini homepage) in Cyworld. In eight weeks the campaign generated 5 million visits to the page, fifty thousand "friends," and over fifty thousand pizza orders placed through the mini-hompy. Other brands have had similar success: Motorola got sixty-one thousand people to clip images of the pink Razr phone for use on their own pages, and almost half a million did the same for the South Korean film *Typhoon,* an action thriller that draws its drama from the tension between North and South Korea.

### When Brands Should Use Social Networks

As compelling as these examples are, branding on social networks isn't for everyone. This is only one way to connect with people who've entered the murky

center of the funnel. Should you use social networking sites to talk with your prospective customers?
Here's our advice:

- *Verify that your customers are in social networks.* If
  half of them are in social networks, then using
  those networks for marketing makes sense.
  Age makes all the difference here. Brands that
  appeal to consumers ages thirteen to twenty-
  three *must* engage in social networks because
  their customers are already there, while those
  with a market between twenty-four to thirty-
  five are likely to be successful with this strategy. As networks like Facebook reach out to
  embrace older people, other brands can begin
  to pursue this strategy, too.

- *Move forward if people love your brand.* Brands
  like Victoria's Secret, Adidas, Jeep, Target, and
  Apple have loyal followers who will friend
  them. A company like Sears without such avid
  brand enthusiasts will have to think and work a
  little harder—focusing on its Craftsman tools
  brand, for example.

- *See what's out there already.* Popular brands inevitably spawn friend pages and networks even
  before the company gets involved. For example,

the Mountain Dew addicts group on MySpace, not authorized by the company, has almost five thousand members. The existence of groups like this shouldn't discourage brands—making friends with them will help you get your own group off the ground. We think Barack Obama's campaign, for example, missed an opportunity when it insisted on shutting down Joe Anthony's Barack Obama profile on MySpace, which had garnered over thirty thousand friends, rather than finding a way to work with him.

- *Create a presence that encourages interaction.* Your fans on MySpace or Facebook want to connect with you. How will you enable that? How will you respond to wall postings? And what interactive elements—wallpaper, badges, widgets—will you provide so people can spread your brand and its messages? Visitors to your page already have some relationship with your brand—how will you help them go deeper into the funnel and influence others? You'll need staff responsible for programming the page and responding to comments, just as if it were part of your Web site. Then prime the pump with a little advertising to your targeted audience, and watch people spread your messages.

Many messages are not quite so easy to spread as the ones marketers are putting on Facebook and MySpace. If you're ready to make a longer-term commitment to your customers—and especially if your brand isn't quite as catchy as a *Typhoon* trailer—then it may be time to look at another way to talk with the groundswell: blogging.

## Case Study

## HP: Talking with Customers Through Blogging

HP has a marketing problem. It sells hundreds of different products. Dozens of types of printers. Cameras. Flat-panel TVs. Every kind of computer, from low-cost notebooks for consumers to huge enterprise-class servers. Lots and lots of software. And billons of dollars' worth of services. All these products are sold to a diverse set of customers—from the largest corporations, to small businesses, to millions of individual consumers around the world.

Many of HP's products are complex, and buyers need help as they reach the middle of the funnel. Advertising or press releases are futile when selling these types of products. Buyers need product details with a human face to help them along. That's why blogging fills a need at HP.

HP decided not to have a single corporate blog, like GM's FastLane, but a variety from all over the company. As the number of bloggers grew, however, HP needed to harness the enthusiasm without allowing chaos to reign. This job of herding the cats fell to Alison Watterson, editor in chief of HP's rich and information-packed Web site. The result was a short, straightforward blogging policy and a course that would-be bloggers could take to keep them within the guardrails. HP's blogging policy includes such commonsensical but better-not-violate gems as "Include your name and position [in blogs and comments] . . . and write in the first person" and this one that made the lawyers happy: "Your blog must comply with financial disclosure laws, regulations and requirements."

Ironically, these rules made blogging spread because now the corporation had blessed it. And HP began to reap the benefits.

## HP's Blogging Paid Off

HP now has nearly fifty executive blogs, on topics from storage and mobility to small businesses. If you're interested in specific types of products or HP's approach to a particular market, there's probably a blog for you.

While the blogs generate traffic, awareness is not the most important benefit. The benefit is that HP can now *respond* to its customers in the middle of the funnel. The dialogue is frequent and diverse with lots of updates, as bloggers respond to what they hear from their own customers, or from comments on the blog. These blogs generate trust because they're personal statements from the executives. And they stimulate discussion among other buyers and bloggers because HP is an active participant in the blogosphere. The total effect is to influence the mass of HP's customers who are blog readers.

A typical example is what happened when Microsoft released Windows Vista. Many customers began to experience printing problems—reports began to circulate on the Web that Vista printer drivers were not working. Then Vince Ferraro, an HP vice president who heads worldwide marketing for HP's LaserJet printers, explained how to solve the Vista problems on his blog. This really opened up communication. Twenty-six blog readers posted comments and questions (sample: "Does this also work for inkjet printers?"). Ferraro responded to these comments, both with comments on his own original post and with a second blog post with lots more detail. As other bloggers linked to the Vista LaserJet post, it rose to become the top result on Google in a search for "HP Vista printer problems." Imagine the hundreds of support calls and unhappy customer complaints nipped in the bud when they read the blog post. Imagine, also, the amount of ink and toner HP sold by keeping those printers humming on the new operating system. By talking with a few customers, Vince Ferraro had responded to thousands of others with similar problems.

Eric Kintz, a thirty-eight-year-old marketing VP and blogger at HP, who was named one of the top ten next-generation marketers by *Brandweek,* explains the value this way: "A lot of our customers look at how much we 'get' this new space. *Fortune* 500 companies need to adapt to this world, and they look to technology partners to help them drive this transformation. If HP impresses just one decision maker at a company this size, the result could unlock tens of millions of dollars of consulting and IT services revenue."

Blogs also allow companies like HP to react appropriately to the blogosphere itself. For example, in August 2006, Sun Microsystems CEO Jonathan Schwartz put this post on his blog after buying cardboard cutouts of HP's founders:

When presented with the opportunity to purchase the likeness of Bill Hewlett and Dave Packard, it having made the trek from the printer ink section of a San Jose Office Depot, our friends at HP elected not to honor their founders. So out of respect for HP's legacy, the fine folks in Sun's marketing team decided to acquire the artwork. Bill and Dave are absolute legends, held in the deepest respect by all of us at Sun. We were honored at the opportunity . . .

With nearly 25% of Solaris downloads requested onto HP's servers, we know their customers really want the partnership, and we're happy to oblige.

Solaris is Sun's operating system. The post was accompanied by a photo of the HP founders wearing a "Sun Solaris" T-shirt. Now this kind of trash talking is silly, admittedly, but it creates a problem. HP's CEO can't respond without looking petty. A press release would seem totally defensive. But in the catty world of Silicon Valley gossip, some response was necessary. So Eric Kintz responded with this blog post:

We strongly value our humble beginnings and the vision of our innovative founders. You can find portraits of Bill and Dave in our lobby; we retained their offices in the condition they were in when they left them and keep them open to everyone here at HP (in the middle of the labs). We also embarked in the last years on a significant effort to preserve the garage on Addison Avenue, where it all began for us and for Silicon Valley. I never met Bill or Dave, but I bet neither of them would have approved paying thousands for representations of themselves.

As for . . . comments on HP-UX, I thought I would share the real story [the last two words are hyperlinked information about the success of HP-UX, HP's system that competes with Sun's Solaris].

Result: the news stories that followed quoted this response and were balanced; Sun's little PR gibe didn't blow up into a full-fledged PR distraction. Decision makers—buyers making decisions about Solaris versus HP-UX—would have had only Sun's CEO's comments about how HP had lost its edge. Now Eric Kintz had presented the other side of the dialogue, by talking *with* his customers.

Companies often ask us about the ROI of blogging. After studying blogs for years, we came up with the model shown in the box "ROI of an executive's blog", based on a high-end blog like GM's FastLane. Technology is *not* the main source of costs; executive education and time are. And the payoff comes down the road, after the blog has developed a following. But because blogs generate high visibility, answer customers' questions, head off PR problems, and eventually lead to insight through customer feed-back, they *do* generate significant ROI.

## Should You Blog?

We get more questions about blogging than any other groundswell technology. And it's not just in America—on a recent trip to Brazil, nearly every

## ROI of an Executive's Blog

In this analysis we assume a single high-level executive blog for a large company, similar to GM's FastLane. Costs include technology, training, and content. Content and training costs account for executives' time. Costs are typical estimates for a large company; many would be lower for smaller companies with a lower profile. All numbers rounded to the nearest thousand.

| Start-up costs | Costs |
| --- | --- |
| Planning and development | $25K |
| Training for blogging executive | 10K |
| **Ongoing costs (annual)** | |
| Blogging platform | 25K |
| Brand-monitoring service | 50K |
| IT support | 3K |
| Content production, including executive time | 150K |
| Review and redirection | 20K |
| *Total costs, year one* | *$283K* |

Again, for benefits we assume a large company blog. Estimates are taken from the FastLane blog. Benefits do not directly account for sales decisions driven from blog readership.

| Benefit analysis (annual) | Value of benefit |
|---|---|
| Advertising value: visibility/traffic (estimate 7,500 daily page views at a $2.50 cost per thousand) | $7K |
| PR value; press stories about/driven from blog content (estimate 24 stories at value of $10K each) | 240K |
| Word-of-mouth value: referring posts on other medium- to high-profile blogs (estimate 370 posts at value of $100 each) | 37K |
| Support value: support calls avoided because of information on blog (estimate 50 daily support calls avoided at $5.50 per call) | 69K |
| Research value: customer insights (estimate comments/feedback equivalent to 5 focus groups at $8K each) | 40K |
| *Total benefits, year one* | *$393K* |

CEO we met with was asking about blogging. No matter what your company does, whom it sells to, or what parts of the world you do business in, people are blogging about your product. As HP found out, your competitors are probably blogging or thinking about blogging. What starts on blogs can rapidly spread to mainstream media.

But before you dive into the blogosphere, ask yourself this question: do I really want to do this?

For example, we recently spoke with Carol Meyers, the CMO at Unica, a company that provides software and services that automate marketing processes. Unica put a lot of effort behind a blog that Carol launched with high hopes in August 2006. In an attempt to reach out as broadly as possible to its marketing customers, Unica tapped a number of guest writer-moderators from inside and outside the company. "We would focus on a topic within marketing every month; we had a little editorial calendar," she explains. "But it got to the point, every month we had to spin somebody up," that is, explain the system to a new contributor. The blog lacked a consistent voice, which we believe made it harder to build an audience, even as it created management challenges for Carol. So the company shut the effort down after a little more than one full year, with a very honest last post in which Carol owned up to fact that the investment needed to maintain the blog wasn't paying off.

Contrast this story with another business-to-business blog from a company called Emerson Process Management, which makes automation systems for manufacturers. Jim Cahill, in Emerson's marketing communications group, is the company's chief blogger at www.emersonprocessxperts.com. Unless you're a plant manager and automation buyer, we're sure you'll find most of Jim's posts pretty boring. But for process automation buyers, these tales from the front lines of process automation are war stories—they can relate, and the stories prove Emerson knows what it's doing. And while Jim frequently features experts from Emerson as guest bloggers, the blog is a big part of his job, and filling it up two or three times a week takes about 30 percent of his time. And it's working—Jim gets three to five contacts a week through the blog, contacts representing early leads that can be worth millions of dollars to his salespeople as they sell huge process automation systems.

What accounts for the difference in these two stories? A couple of things. First of all, Jim was excited to blog and enjoyed the attention, while Carol was continually managing others to contribute; her guest authors didn't really own the blog. This lack of ownership shows through—remember, your readers are *people*, even in a business-to-business setting, and they want to connect with another person.

Also, it's important to note that Jim knew his audience—people who buy and use process automation systems. Carol's audience—marketers—was probably too broad. One important product at Unica is in marketing analytics—if the company starts a new blog with that focus, it could be more successful the second time around.

## *Tips for Successful Blogging*

The prerequisite for starting a blog is to want to engage in dialogue with your customers. Some companies have a CEO or senior executive who is aching to say what's on his or her mind—those are good candidates. Like Rick Clancy, Sony Electronics' EVP of communications who also blogs for the company, they may be nervous, but they have the drive. Nobody can be forced to do this. Blogging is too personal, and requires too much effort, to be crammed down anybody's throat. The result of that, inevitably, will look and feel lame, and it's worse than not having a blog at all.

If you or your company is ready to seriously consider entering the blogosphere, remember to start with *people* and *objectives*. If you know whom you want to reach and exactly what you want to accomplish, then you're far more likely to succeed. What remains is to implement the strategy and technology appropriately to accomplish your objectives. Here are ten suggestions for beginning the dialogue, based on our experience:

1. *Start by listening.* A small knot of people at a cocktail party are conversing. Would you

walk up to them and just start talking? Or would you listen, first, and see how you can join their conversation? The blogosphere is the same. Listen to what's being said out there before you dive in. Monitor the blogs in your industry, from competitors, pundits, and other influencers. For a more comprehensive view, hire a brand-monitoring service like Nielsen BuzzMetrics or TNS Cymfony.

2. *Determine a goal for the blog.* Will you focus on announcing new products? Supporting existing customers? Responding to news stories? Making your executives seem more human? Choose goals so you know where you are going.

3. *Estimate the ROI.* Using a spreadsheet, determine how you think the blog will pay off and what it will cost. This is especially helpful in gaining buy-in from other functions throughout the company and in disciplining your thinking.

4. *Develop a plan.* Some blogs—like Jonathan Schwartz's at Sun—have one author. Others, like GM's FastLane, feature several. (If one person doesn't have enough time or content

to post every week or so, this is a good idea.) You'll also need to determine whether you'll have a single company blog, like George Wright's at Blendtec, or a policy that enables blogging to spread to many employees and many different blogs, like HP's.

5. *Rehearse.* Write five or ten posts *before* allowing them to go live. This is your spring training—when you find out what it's going to be like without all the flashbulbs going off. It also allows you to explore what sorts of topics you'll cover. If you can't write five practice posts, you're not ready for the big leagues.

6. *Develop an editorial process.* Who, if anyone, needs to review posts? (The general counsel? The CMO? A copy editor?) Who's your backup if these people aren't available? This process needs to be built lightweight for speed because you'll sometimes want to post quickly to respond to events and news items.

7. *Design the blog and its connection to your site.* You'll have to decide how—and even whether—to feature your blog on the company's home page, depending on how central you'd like it to be to the company's image.

Your design and the way you link the blog to your site will communicate just how official this point of view is.

8. *Develop a marketing plan so people can find the blog.* Start with traditional methods—a press release to get coverage from trade magazines in your area, for example, and emails to your customers introducing the blog. You may also want to buy words on search engines. But remember that the blogosphere is a conversation—you're talking with people, not shouting at them. You can leverage the traffic of the popular blogs you identified in step 1: include links to those blogs in your posts, and post comments on them to lead people back to you. The text of your posts will also help—by using the names of your company and your products in the titles and text of posts, you will make it easier for people to find your blog in search engines.

9. *Remember, blogging is more than writing.* To be a successful blogger, you should start by monitoring the blogosphere and responding to what else is out there, not behaving as if you are in a vacuum. And remember that your blog will have comments—if it doesn't,

there's no dialogue, and you're no longer talking with people as they make decisions about your products—and that's the whole point. Finally, many corporate blogs use moderation, vetting comments to make sure offensive and off-topic chatter doesn't mar the blog. This takes time, too, but you should do it. You can delegate the tasks of monitoring other blogs and responding to and moderating comments, but someone has to do them, or your blog won't be part of the dialogue.

10. *Final advice: be honest.* People expect a blog to be a genuine statement of a person's opinion. This doesn't mean you can't be positive about your company, but you need to respond as a real person. Sometimes bad things happen to good people and good companies—like Dell's laptop batteries catching fire. Dell's first post on the topic actually linked to a picture of the "flaming notebook" and included this frank admission: "We . . . are still investigating the cause." This was followed up by posts about how to get defective batteries replaced, once the company had decided to offer replacements. A company that responds honestly, even when thing go wrong, boosts its credibility.

Even with all the focus on blogging, it's a mistake to assume this is the only way, or even the best way, to talk with the groundswell. George Wright of Blendtec found another way. And Procter & Gamble, as you'll see in the next case, found a unique way to use communities to talk to a very challenging collection of customers.

## Case Study

### Procter's & Gamble's Beinggirl.com: Talking with a Community

Let's talk about tampons.

What's that you say? You don't *want* to talk about tampons? Well, now you can understand the challenge Bob Arnold has at Procter & Gamble (P&G).

Bob is part of the team tasked with marketing feminine care products to young girls. At age thirty, he's had only one employer, P&G, and had previously worked on Internet sites for P&G's cleaning products aimed at women. But feminine care products are a whole other level of difficulty.

The consumers in this case are utterly resistant to messages about the product category. (Even more than you don't want to talk about tampons, an eleven-year old girl *really* doesn't want to talk about them—or listen to a commercial when her brother is in the room.) The consumers are surrounded by parents who object to marketing messages directed at their children. In fact, these consumers and their parents are often making decisions based on discussions that P&G can't be a part of. And in this market, once a consumer makes a choice, she probably sticks with it for a long time.

Bob Arnold and the team at Procter & Gamble's femcare group needed a new way to speak to their consumers. Traditional advertising was problematic —shouting doesn't work so well when people are embarrassed to listen. So Bob and his team conceived a new approach—solve the girls' problems, instead of marketing to them. This was the genesis of being-girl.com.

## What's Beinggirl.com?

Beinggirl.com is not a community site about tampons. (Who would visit that?) It's about *everything* that young girls deal with. Nearly half of girls ages twelve to fifteen are in social networks, and three out of ten react to content in, for example, blog comments and discussion forums. So Bob set out to create a site that had categories girls would be interested in, as opposed to those that would sell product. "We own this sort of growing-up part that people are too scared to touch," he told us. "We've really tried to create a community around that."

What does this mean? It means girls can share their most embarrassing experiences, like this one:

**"Have you ever done it?"**
I was taking a walk with my crush and we were talking about a lot of different things. Eventually he started talking about sports, but I wasn't listening because I was too busy checking him out. Then I heard him say, "Have you ever done it?" I responded with, "No, not yet, because I want to find and fall in love with the right person first." He looked at me and said, "I was talking about snowboarding, remember?!" I thought he had asked if I'd ever had sex before!

What does this have to do with tampons? Nothing. What does it have to do with being a young girl? Everything! This entry, by the way, got 19,331 votes from other girls on the site, making it the top submission in the "Laugh out loud" section.

Another popular part of the site features a psychologist, Dr. Iris Prager, who will answer your questions, no matter how embarrassing. Here's a typical example from "Ask Iris."

## How should you react when you get your first period

Hey, Iris,

When you get your period for the first time, how should you react?

Jody

Dear Jody,

I think you should celebrate . . . this is a huge "rite of passage" in your life. You should tell your mom first and let her set the tone. It's a really important event in your life and you'll always remember just how it happened. You can also click <u>here</u> to find good information on what to expect when you get your period.

Good Luck, Iris, for beinggirl.com, brought to you by Always pads & pantiliners and Tampax tampons

Notice how subtle the branding is. What's delivered here is big dose of sensitivity with a small dollop of information and a tiny brand message. This really is talking *with* your customers.

Iris also answers other favorites like "Will a shark attack me if I swim in the ocean during my period?" (answer: it's better to be careful and wear a tampon) and "How can I get along better with my mom?" (don't always try to have the last word). Some are about puberty and health, and some are not. But every post has that little brand tag at the end.

Bob Arnold and his team know their market. Beinggirl.com features music through a partnership with Sony BMG (no money changed hands—Sony likes the audience, and P&G likes the content). It includes sharing and games, the kind of stuff that girls connect with. It's carefully monitored to prevent people from exchanging phone numbers, real names, or email addresses, which keeps girls safe. And of course, it includes information about periods and feminine care products—in an environment where girls can check it out without officially going to a "tampon site."

Is it working? Well, Bob says beinggirl.com now attracts more than 2 million visitors a month worldwide. Traffic in 2007 was up over 150 percent versus the previous year. That's a record any media site would envy, and this is a site set up by a consumer packaged goods company!

How did beinggirl.com get there? Procter & Gamble cleverly gives the site a little boost. First of all, it's featured in the kits that the company distributes for health classes around the country. That's how a lot of girls hear about it. Secondly, once a week, P&G emails girls who sign up, to remind them about the site and bring them back. And finally, the company includes a free sample area—fill out a few questions, and P&G will figure out what you need and send you a few.

Take a look at what P&G did here. Because young girls resist messages about the company's products, its marketers were pretty much locked out of the funnel. To become part of the dialogue among young girls, Procter & Gamble created a social network. And because it solved customers' problems, instead of its own, the customers were willing to share. Add subtle brand messages and free samples, and P&G was able to become part of the dialogue from which it had previously been excluded.

### Measuring the Payoff of Beinggirl.com

Is there a company that understands the value of media better than P&G? This is the company that practically invented the soap opera and spends $7.9 billion per year to advertise its products worldwide. But media is one thing. Community is another. Community is better.

According to P&G's internal math, beinggirl.com is four times as effective as advertising in reaching its target consumers. That's why P&G has expanded beinggirl.com to twenty-nine countries in Europe, Asia, and South America. "The world is getting smaller," Bob Arnold explains. "There are more similarities between girls then there are differences. The things that excite a girl in the U.S. are similar to [those that excite] a girl in China or Japan."

Let's do a little math on the value of beinggirl.com.

One purpose of beinggirl.com is to introduce girls to P&G products. Girls tend to stick with the same brand throughout their lives, so each of those girls could end up as a woman spending $5 a month for feminine care products for forty years or so. That's $2,400 per girl. Assume a profit margin of 20 percent, and each girl who picks Tampax and Always is worth $480 to the company.

We estimate that a site like this, now being run internationally, costs about $3 million a year to run. That means the site has to persuade only 6,250 girls to use its products to break even. Even a 1 percent conversion rate of beinggirl.com's traffic is three times higher than that breakeven point.

Beinggirl.com has now expanded to include subtle messages about Herbal Essences shampoo and Venus razors—as long as the girls are there, might as well help 'em out with other personal care products. And based on the subtle approach, we doubt if the traffic will suffer.

Bob Arnold's success has had another side effect. P&G has instituted a "reverse mentoring" program. Internet whizzes like him now tutor the senior executives on how the groundswell will affect their brands. Not a bad spot for a thirty-year-old in a big, traditional company.

## When Communities Make Sense

Procter & Gamble took a big risk with beinggirl.com and reaped a big reward. Should your company do the same? Before deciding, you need to do a little risk-reward calculation on your own.

First, figure out whether your market really is a community—or could be one. Assess the community readiness of the target group—larger-than-average numbers of social network members indicate a higher likelihood of a successful community. Then take the next step—ask yourself whether *your* customers really are a community.

Mini owners were pleased to join a community based on their affinity to a car. Other groups that might look to a community would include groups where people naturally support each other, like disease sufferers. Fans of sports teams also form communities. But there's almost certainly no Grape-Nuts community and no cable subscriber community—these groups have little to bond over. Some companies will be able to think more broadly—as P&G did, creating a "young girl" community instead of a feminine care products site. But unless you can define a credible community around your customers' passions or pain points, you'll get nowhere.

Second, if your customers naturally join communities, they have probably already joined the communities already out there. P&G's beinggirl.com is actually in competition with other social networking sites aimed at young girls, like piczo.com and flip.com. It's always cheaper to sponsor such a site than to try to build your own, although you give up control. The key is, P&G defined a community around an issue that attracts girls' attention—the problems of growing up. Another generic girl community would have ended up competing with—and losing out to—Piczo, Barbie Girls, or other popular sites for young girls.

Third, once you've figured out whether you can form a community and what the central attraction will be, ask yourself these questions: What are we going to get out of this? How will talking with this community benefit us? With P&G's prospective lifetime value of each girl representing $2,400 worth of merchandise, the community makes sense. Unless you can do the math and generate a similarly positive outcome by advertising to your community, you'll be going to an awful lot of trouble for a dubious outcome.

Finally, do not continue unless you can support the community for the long term. Communities are cheap to create—you can create one for free at ning. com, for example—but to create an effective community, you must constantly support and maintain it. Communities need care and feeding—with content, new features, and redesigns—to stay relevant and successful. Pulling the plug will have a negative impact on your customers. So it's best not to proceed unless you're certain you'll get the benefits you're looking for.

## Talking with the Groundswell: What It Means to You

We've now seen four ways to talk with the groundswell—viral videos, social networks, blogs, and communities. Which will work for you?

Well, that depends on what your communications problem is. And that, in turn, depends on what your customers are doing in the middle of the funnel.

Do you have an *awareness* problem (people don't know about you)? Maybe you have a *word-of-mouth* problem (you need people to talk to each other). Or it could be that you have a *complexity* problem (you have complicated messages to communicate). Finally, if your customers are buried deep in the funnel where you can't reach them at all, you have an *accessibility* problem.

Each of the techniques we described in this chapter solves one of those problems.

Viral videos are best for punching through the noise—the awareness problem. They're great for unknowns like Blendtec. There's just one problem: you need a brilliant idea. Remember, people don't choose to watch commercials—while they *do* choose to watch (and recommend) videos like "Will It Blend?" and "Greg the Architect." Just remember that (if you succeed), you're about to enter into a conversation with hundreds of thousands of people who read the Web address at the end of your video (you did remember the Web address, didn't you?). You need to be ready, as Blendtec was, to convert all that interest into action and consideration as you suck those people into the funnel.

Social networks are the best solution for word-of-mouth problems. Word of mouth is critical for clothes, movies, TV shows—these are fashion products. It's also critical for cars. If you want to be hot, and have people talking about how hot you are, then MySpace and Facebook are for you—just don't forget to include the viral elements that your fans can share. These venues are also great for anything youth and campus focused, as Ernst & Young and Adidas have proved. The key is to be there—to respond to what your customers are saying—so you can help them through the funnel.

Big companies, technology companies, and lots of other companies have a complexity problem—they have multiple sets of customers, or they have high-consideration, complex products or services. Blogs help solve this problem. Complexity is a big issue in the middle of the funnel, since that's where decisions get made, and complexity hampers decisions. Financial services, technology, cars, home improvement, and fashion are all categories that involve consideration of complex options. Not only can blogs help with this consideration, but they can also reassure people before, during, and after the sale. And as an added bonus, blog posts often get featured in mainstream media and Web searches, improving awareness for complex products.

Finally, some customers are just stubbornly insistent on depending on each other, not on listening to you. For you, they represent an accessibility problem. If they insist on depending on each other, the best you can do is create an environment where they can do that. That's a community, and you should either create one for them or join one they've created for themselves. Just remember that maintaining a community is a long-term commitment.

## How Starting a Conversation Will Change the Way You Think About Marketing

The transition from shouting to conversation will challenge your marketing department. It's a fundamental change in attitude.

Marketers are used to shouting and then listening for the echo. This is an awareness tactic, and it's fine for the big end of the funnel. Awareness remains crucially important, so don't expect the groundswell to change that part of your marketing.

It's what comes next—the conversation—that marketers must prepare for.

You're about to become involved in the consideration process. This process is messy. It includes people, comments, and feedback. It's not a shout-once kind of a thing.

Marketing departments will need to develop new skills to listen, and then respond to, feedback from the groundswell. These are skills that companies have, but they're usually part of consultative selling or customer support. So prepare by getting the marketing people in your organization to know how to respond to customers as individuals. These people will be responding to posts on social networks, blog comments, community activity, and videos on user-generated sites. Think of them as moderators to the conversation.

These staff cost money, certainly. But remember that each response is visible on the Web. Your response to each individual is visible to many. Like Dan Black's answers for Ernst & Young employment queries, Eric Kintz's posts on HP server software, and Dr. Iris's advice to young girls, these responses will be read by hundreds of potential customers. That's the value that comes from talking with the groundswell.

Furthermore, remember that conversations require not just listening but responding. It's not about the big bang; it's about constant responsiveness, whether in a blog, a community, or a social network. HP's Vince Ferraro knew he needed a second post to solve his customers' LaserJet problems. You must adopt the same sort of thinking. Campaigns begin and end, but conversations go on forever.

Marketers must also prepare for changes in their agency relationships.

Shouting works well with traditional advertising agencies. One part of the agency creates the shout. Another places it in media. Then, if your agency is any good, you measure the results and see whether you made an impact.

Agencies aren't used to conversations, but some are learning. Carat's Isobar division has proved it can manage—and measure—campaigns on social networks. Edelman's Me2Revolution focuses on social technologies. Despite their early stumbles, we expect agencies to get better at helping clients with these activities. But ask for proof that an agency has managed—and measured—a campaign aimed at the murky social middle of the funnel.

Proof comes from measurement. But marketers and their agencies must now measure results that move well beyond reach and frequency to *engagement*—how far down the funnel your prospect has traveled. While engagement is trickier to measure, it includes tracking navigation paths on your own Web site and comments on your blogs. It also includes measures of buzz and sentiment about your products, metrics we explained in our description of listening in the previous chapter.

If we can leave you with one thought about talking with the groundswell, it's this: the conversation will evolve continuously. Even as the technologies change, the basic conversational nature of those technologies will remain central. If you learn to talk, listen, and respond, you'll master the middle of the funnel.

All the marketing techniques we describe in this chapter tap into word of mouth: talking with the groundswell means stimulating conversation. Word of mouth is a powerful force in the groundswell. You can even use it to generate sales. That's the topic of the next chapter, where we describe how to use the groundswell to energize the sales potential of your best customers.

# Energizing the Groundswell

Jim Noble is a hard-nosed computer security engineer from Georgia. He's a frequent traveler, a real "get-'er-done" kind of a guy, which is why it's so surprising to hear him talk with real enthusiasm about his luggage.

Sit next to him on a plane, and once he wedges his six-foot, three-inch, 300-pound frame into the seat, he'll tell you about his laptop bag. He calls it "an impromptu sales demo." First, you'll hear about how the "pumpkin-vomit-colored" interior (his words) makes it easy to see whether one of those dozens of little computer accessories has been left inside. "There isn't a wasted square centimeter on this bag," he says. And on and on until you ask him to stop.

How did Jim turn into a luggage evangelist? It's because the online store that sold the laptop bag to him, eBags, has figured out how to energize its customers.

Here's his story: after a long month of travel and on the way to a security conference in New York, a key zipper on Jim's laptop bag failed. The folks at eBags replaced it the next day. But that's not what turned Jim from a guy annoyed with his broken luggage into an eBags fan. What energized Jim is that people at eBags actually listened to the review he posted on their Web site, contacted him, and then improved the product, getting the factory in Hong Kong to change the design so the zipper wouldn't break anymore, even after constant punishment by road warriors like Jim.

As an engineer, Jim wants things to be built right. So a company that listens and fixes things, like eBags, gets his attention, his loyalty, and his copious word of mouth.

But eBags isn't just listening, and it's not just talking; it's energizing—finding enthusiast customers and turning them into word-of-mouth machines. And because most people, unlike Jim, don't talk all that much about luggage, eBags gives them the teeniest little push, encouraging them to write reviews on its site. This is energizing, the third level of groundswell thinking.

## What Is Energizing?

In the late 1970s, Faberge Organics shampoo ran a commercial that sticks in the brain of any of us of a certain age. Heather Locklear (yes, it was her) enthused about how the shampoo was so great that "you'll tell two friends, and they'll tell two friends, and so on, and so on, and so on . . ."

It's a marketer's dream.

When political candidates get their supporters riled up and spreading the word, we call it "energizing the base." It's the same with companies and their customers. Energizing the base is a powerful way to use the groundswell to boost your business.

An energized customer like Jim Noble is a viral marketer, spreading brand benefits to his contacts without any cost to the company. Individually, no consumer can achieve the reach of mass media. But word of mouth is a powerful amplifier of brand marketing, achieving results no media campaign can achieve. Word of mouth succeeds because:

- *It's believable.* Testimonials from customers are far more credible than any media source.

- *It's self-reinforcing.* Hear it from one person, and it's intriguing. Hear it from five or ten, even if you didn't know them before, and it has to be true.

- *It's self-spreading.* Just as Heather Locklear said, if a product is worth using, its word of mouth generates more word of mouth in a cascade that's literally exponential.

According to the Word of Mouth Marketing Association (WOMMA), word of mouth "is the most honest form of marketing, building upon people's natural desire to share their experiences with family, friends, and colleagues." It can't be faked, but it can be encouraged, which is why over five hundred marketers attend WOMMA's summit every year.

As we discussed in the previous two chapters, listening to the groundswell generates insights, and talking to the groundswell is effective, but marketers need not stop there. *Energizing* the groundswell means tapping into the power of word of mouth by connecting with, and turning on, your most committed customers, like Jim Noble with his improved laptop bag.

### *Energizing the Base*

According to Forrester surveys, on average, more than one out of six of your customers are blogging, uploading video, and maintaining Web sites. Are these people talking about your product? If they love your product, they *may* be. They're talking about something, in any case.

But the people who create content are only part of the story. One in four people online are reacting to content by commenting on blogs, participating in forums, or posting ratings and reviews. Nearly half are reading blogs and watching videos created by others.

Now suppose you could encourage people to write about your product or to upload video about your product. All of a sudden, the other people consuming socially created content will start hearing about it. A little bit of effort could result in a lot of impact. And the impact will be more powerful because people believe other *people* more than *media*.

## The Value of an Energized Customer

We told you this book would put ROI in the discussion of how to tap groundswell phenomena. Well, what's the value of an energized customer?

The definitive answer to this question comes from Fred Reichheld in his book *The Ultimate Question: Driving Good Profits and True Growth*, one of the most influential business books of recent years. The ultimate question the book discusses is this: "How likely is it that you would recommend [company name/product name] to a friend or colleague?" Customers answer on a scale from 0 to 10. Subtract the detractors (those who answered 0 to 6) from the promoters (those who answered 9 or 10), and you get a Net Promoter Score (NPS). Fred Reichheld's exhaustive research proves that the NPS correlates with sustainable growth across many industries.

Jim Noble, the eBags' customer we met earlier, is a great example of a promoter. How much is a promoter like Jim worth? Well, that depends on how much of your business comes from word of mouth. For example, at Dell, 25 percent of new customers said they chose Dell from another customer's referral. Given the value of Dell's customers ($210 each), Fred Reichheld estimates the value of each promoter's positive word of mouth at $42.[1] Get that customer to generate twice as many positive contacts, and you double that return. That's the value of energizing.

There's one caveat. As Fred told us, "The value varies based on which customers come to you based on your reputation and referrals . . . and how much comes from advertising." But Fred is unequivocal about generating energized customers as being the best sign that a business is healthy and can grow. Assuming you have energized customers, amping up the word of mouth is definitely good business, with a value that increases for those with more business from referrals and a higher average purchase for those referred customers.

There's another measure of the value of word of mouth, and it's this: you can actually buy it.

A Massachusetts company, BzzAgent, will be happy to sell you a word-of-mouth program. You sign up, and it sends some of its three hundred thousand "volunteer brand evangelists" your product or coupons for your product. If your product is poor, BzzAgents won't talk about it. But if they like it, they will.

Essentially, BzzAgent has recruited more than a quarter of a million people to evaluate products and put them on retainer, paid in coupons for coffee and the thrill of trying out new stuff. And those BzzAgent recruits talk to an average of sixty other people on each campaign.

How much does this cost? For a 10,000-agent campaign, the cost is $280,000. And while some find BzzAgent's tactics controversial, it does seem to work. (BzzAgent conducted over three hundred campaigns between 2005 and 2007.) So based on BzzAgent's math, an energized consumer will cost you $28.

This is great. But energizing your own customers can work even better than working with BzzAgents. BzzAgents only review what they're told to review. In contrast, your customers self-select because they like your products, and they keep talking about those products for years. That's why it's worth it to energize them.

## Techniques for Energizing Enthusiasts

So having absorbed the wisdom of Fred Reichheld and BzzAgent, let's say you've decided to take advantage of the passion of your most enthusiastic customers—the Jim Nobles in your customer base. You'd like to make it easy for them to spread the word about your product. You'd like to get them charged up so they'll tell everyone they know. What should you do?

Based on our interviews with companies that have succeeded in this endeavor, there are three basic techniques for connecting with your brand's enthusiasts:

1. *Tap into customers' enthusiasm with ratings and reviews.* This works best for retail companies and others with direct customer contact. Our first case study, eBags, shows how this works in detail.

2. *Create a community to energize your customers.* This works best if your customers are truly passionate about your product and have an affinity for each other, especially in business-to-business settings. Our second case study shows how this worked for email marketing service company Constant Contact.

3. *Participate in and energize online communities of your brand enthusiasts.* Our third case study examines how this worked for the Lego company as it energized its most enthusiastic adult customers.

## Case Study

### Ebags: Energizing with Ratings and Reviews

The SVP of marketing at eBags, Peter Cobb, appears to be filled with boundless enthusiasm. Years ago he overcame cancer, and now he's dedicated his career to selling luggage. His company is an unalloyed success story, still posting a 30 percent annual growth rate after eight years of selling luggage, backpacks, and handbags on the Internet. But what's most interesting about eBags, and what Peter likes to talk about most, is how the company turns its customers into an incredibly powerful asset. "We were just blown away by the level of detail people include," says Peter, which is why their ratings and reviews are now front and center on the site.

For example, suppose you've decided to buy a carry-on that doubles as a backpack for that European vacation you've been planning. This purchase might be $50, $100, or $200, but it's far more important than that. If the bag fails to perform, you'll be suffering pain and frustration in a foreign country, which has to be one of the inner circles in Dante's vision of hell. So you'd better be sure it's right.

In three or four clicks on eBags, you learn not only that the eBags Weekender Convertible, at $59.99, was a best seller but that "1151 of 1185 customers said they would buy this product again." Wow! First of all, over a thousand customers took the time to give it a thumbs-up or a thumbs-down. And second, 97 percent of them gave it a thumbs-up. That's pretty reassuring, especially since those buyers rated it at least a 9 on a 10-point scale for features like appearance, durability, and price / value.

So who writes those reviews? Here's one, from a woman in Portland, Oregon, who doesn't travel much but used the bag to go on vacation:

My husband purchased this bag first. It was very nice so I bought mine. Like someone reviewed, this is the bag to walk around European cobble roads since wheeled luggages are completely useless in such an environment. In my last trip, I used a regular carry-on wheeler for a check-in bag and took this bag as a carry-on. It fits in the compartment pretty nicely because it is very flexible without wheels. Since the airline companies more tightly restrict the weight of check-in luggages recently, it seems to be the best if you have two carry-on size bags. (Larger luggages may go over the weight limit once [they are] packed.) I recommend this bag especially if you are thinking of buying the second carry-on bag.

Thanks, whoever you are. That bit about the cobblestones is a good point—might not have thought of that. Two carry-on bags, good idea. And you bought a second one after your husband bought one; that's reassuring. But what about the people who didn't like it? It takes only a second to sort those reviews from worst to best. Then you learn what David, from Jamaica Plain, Massachusetts, said:

This is an excellent item, but it was too small for my needs so I returned it. I'm a big guy, so I need room for my big clothes. The quality of the material is excellent, the zippers seem very durable, and the tuck away straps and waist belt are of [superior] quality [compared] to many similar bags. There were a few aspects of the bag that I did not like: 1) It does not [expand] at all, so using it as a larger, checked bag is not an option. 2) The front pocket has zip pockets and pen holders which makes its storage ability less flexible. 3) It looks like a backpack even when the straps are zipped in. 4) The compression straps do not go around the entire bag. In the end I bought a Rick Steves bag for more money that is made of lower quality material but holds much more (and can still be checked). The weekender convertible is an exceptional bag if you are a talented packer able to bring only the necessities.

OK, so David didn't like it. But maybe he's just not a good packer; plus, his clothes are really big. If that's the worst that people can come up with, we're sold.

One click and we're happy. And eBags' Peter Cobb, who's clearly a hell of a salesman, didn't have to sell us at all. His *customers* did.

## How Ebags Energized its Customers

Buying luggage is a touchy-feely kind of purchase. This isn't like buying books on amazon.com; you don't have to see books to buy them. It's an intimate relationship we have with our luggage. Our *stuff* goes in there. You don't trust your stuff to just anything. So it would seem that an online seller of luggage would be at a disadvantage to a luggage store, where you can see the bag and talk to a salesperson. The people behind eBags knew this, so they implemented ratings and reviews on their site to make up for the insecurity that comes from not being able to touch the bag before you buy it.

Now, unlike some of the other examples in this book, there is no such thing as a luggage community. People don't get together over coffee and talk about luggage. There are no luggage enthusiasts (and if there are, you don't want to meet them). But people do care a lot about luggage, because that luggage holds their stuff. So when, twenty-one days after a bag ships, eBags sends an email suggesting that the customer review the product, 22 percent respond. eBags is tapping into people's desire to react to content, which is far easier than trying to get luggage consumers to become luggage narrators, blogging about their luggage experiences or uploading luggage videos to YouTube.

Business travelers are in an upscale segment that overindexes on participation in all online social activities. What's the right groundswell strategy for these folks? Energize their desire to create and react to what they see, and use the comments they create to influence those who like to read content from others. In other words, ratings and reviews are a perfect strategy for a company that targets business travelers.

What you see at eBags is the groundswell at work. People want to depend on other people. Peter Cobb knew that. All he had to do was to make it easy for them to talk, and they did. And like so many groundswell phenomena, the eBags site builds on itself. You read the reviews, you buy the product, you use it, and then you figure, "Hey, why don't I contribute to help the next guy?"

This is energizing the groundswell the easy way. There's no need to set up accounts, maintain profile pages, or weed out cyberstalkers. And it works.

### Benefits of Ratings and Reviews

At eBags, the return on ratings and reviews is highly measurable. Reviews increase the buy rate. It's hard to know just how much ratings improve the buy rate because there is no control case, no ebags.com without reviews. But our surveys show that 76 percent of customers use online reviews to help them make purchases. In fact, even though only 25 percent of ecommerce sites have ratings and reviews, 96 percent of the sites that have them rate them as an effective merchandising tactic. Sucharita Mulpuru, a Forrester analyst who concentrates on online retailing, recommends including reviews unequivocally: "Any site that allows the purchase of commodity products should collect and expose reviews."

Bazaarvoice, a company that makes ratings and reviews systems for Web sites, has done case studies with controls. Visitors to Petco's pet supplies site who browsed specifically by highest-rated products were 49 percent more likely to buy. Although it's difficult to make direct comparisons (probably those who read reviews are generally more interested, which contributes to their willingness to purchase), it's clear that ratings and reviews generate more purchases.

Based on this, we can compute the ROI of ratings and reviews at a site like eBags (see box). Using very conservative estimates of increases in business, we estimate that a $200,000 investment in ratings will yield $400,000 in profit the first year, and more in subsequent years. That's double your investment back in one year. Not bad.

Web executives sometimes see this potential but worry about negative reviews. However, our research shows that about 80 percent of reviews tend to be positive. And in fact, the negative reviews are essential to the credibility of the site—without them, the positive reviews just don't seem believable.

## ROI of Ratings and Reviews

Bazaarvoice charges about $25K a year for its system, with an up-front development cost of around $50K. Ratings are most effective with an employee in house analyzing what's coming back from the customers.

## Marketing in the Groundswell

| Cost analysis (first year) | Costs |
|---|---|
| Up-front development cost paid to technology vendor | $50K |
| Yearly ongoing costs paid to technology vendor | 25K |
| Additional yearly ongoing costs at company | 125K |
| *Total costs, year one* | *$200K* |

Assume an online retailer that sells $25m a year, with 10m site visitors and 250K customers per year (a 2.5% conversion rate), and a $100 average transaction. We estimate that ratings increase the conversion rate by 20% and the transaction size for those customers by an average of 10% (many companies exceed this). Assume further that the reviews only boost sales on the top 20% of items, since those will get the most reviews in year one.

| Profit analysis (first year) | After ratings and reviews |
|---|---|
| Site visitors | 10m |
| Visitors seeing reviews (20% in year one) | 2m |
| Sales at typical 2.5% conversion, $100 per transaction | $5m |
| Sales with ratings/reviews: 3% conversion, $110 per transaction | $6.6m |

| | |
|---|---|
| Net additional sales because of ratings/reviews | $1.6m |
| *Net additional profit at 25% profit margin* | *$400K* |

But another reason ratings and reviews help, whether positive or negative, is leverage with suppliers. And eBags knows more about the products it sells than the people who manufacture them. It provides a report to every single one of its 370 brands every Monday, telling them not only what's selling but what people think of those products. What offline retailer could do that?

Reinforcing this last point, Peter Cobb told us an interesting story. His site sold a hard-sided bag called the International Traveler. It was popular because it looked sharp. But after getting great reviews for a while, something changed. "I started seeing thumbs-downs," Peter told us. At first, it was one a week, then three a week, and then six a week. People were saying, "I use this bag, and I love the looks. But the second time I used it, the outside cracked." Or "I threw it in a cab and it cracked." Peter decided the company must have changed something in the chemical process used to make the hard shell, and the new shell wasn't standing up to the beating that these bags take in the way that it used to.

The manufacturer denied it. Peter persisted. "No, we haven't changed anything," the manufacturer insisted.

As the negative comments mounted, the manufacturer reversed itself. "They came back and said, 'You were right; there was some type of manufacturing problem. We need to fix this,'" Peter reports. And that fix solved the cracking problem.

In traditional retail, the manufacturer is completely insulated from the end buyer. Returns go back up the supply chain. Macy's has no way to keep track of problems like this, and if it did, doing so could take months to figure out. But eBags has a powerful connection to its customers and knew within a few weeks that something went wrong. By aligning itself with the groundswell, eBags gained power over its suppliers, even as it became a hero to its own customers by fixing the problem.

## Case Study

### Constant Contact: Energizing by Creating a Community

What's the difference between spam and legitimate email?

Simple. Spam is email you don't want.

But on that simple question hangs the success of a company called Constant Contact. Constant Contact is an email marketing company. The focus at Constant Contact is on helping small businesses stay in touch with their own customers. If those customers have provided their email address, the small-business owner can drum up business by sending email newsletters, notes about what's on sale this month, and reminders for people to get their teeth or their chimneys cleaned. But by law (the CAN-SPAM Act), if people get annoyed, they can opt out of the email list. Legitimate email marketers comply with this rule. Spammers often don't.

As Gail Goodman, Constant Contact's CEO, explains, the lion's share of growth at Constant Contact comes from word of mouth. The company encourages this with a referral program—get a friend to sign up, and you get a $30 credit and he gets a $30 credit. Satisfaction is crucial because customers can stop paying the monthly fees at any time and opt out.

So when Gail's head of customer experience, Maureen Royal, proposed creating a community forum where customers could encourage each other, Gail was intrigued. Maureen had already proved that Constant Contact's customers loved to schmooze by assembling them, a dozen or so at a time, at dinners in various cities. Why not let them connect online?

Small-business owners are active participants in the groundswell.

Constant Contact's "ConnectUp!" community launched in 2005, and it worked. ConnectUp! now gets participation from thirteen thousand people, 10 percent of its customers. It's highly active, with over six thousand posts in thirty-nine forums. People are answering each others' questions, encouraging new sign-ups to stick with it, and generating referrals. Constant Contact's forum is, basically, a home for energized customers.

Thirty percent of community members generate referrals. Constant Contact estimates that each referral that turns into a customer generates a lifetime revenue of almost $1,500 (the cost is the $60 credit). Constant Contact's revenues grew 88 percent between 2005 and 2006, beating the previous year's 82 percent growth. This company is on a roll, and energizing its customers in a community is stoking the growth.

To understand why community works to drive revenue for Constant Contact, look first at its customer base. Obviously, they're all online. But small-business people are a perfect target for community. They share common problems—running a company is tough, whether you're a restaurateur or a plumbing supplier. They're mostly not technical or marketing whizzes, so they can use help from those who've puzzled out the right ways to do email. And they like to brag about their successes to each other. So when Constant Contact encouraged them to join the community as they logged into their email marketing tools, many did.

Constant Contact's customers also shared another critical interest: *they didn't want to be seen as spammers.*

The first heated discussion on Constant Contact's newly minted forum concerned spam. And it threatened to get out of hand. Some respondents complained about how the company put their accounts on hold based on too many spam complaints. Others defended Constant Contact, pointing out that its reputation as a legitimate email marketer—not a spammer—depended on this activity. In the end Gail put on a Web seminar explaining the company's policy, and that settled the issue. The Constant Contact community raised an issue, the company responded, and its members went back to sending emails and referring new customers.

Even now the community has a self-supporting feeling. Altruistic motivations are powerful forces here. Kelly Rusk (known in the Constant Contact community as "cardcommunications"), a twenty-three-year-old Canadian woman working as an emarketing specialist, feels good when she gets to answer posts like this:

**BadAndy 80**

That's me, the bad bad spammer . . . I had 6 spam reports out of 2000 emails, which is over the 1/1000 that they consider normal.

I waited on hold for 20 minutes to unfreeze my account and some guy acted like I was a bad guy for having 6. He genuinely sounded MAD at me. I couldn't believe my ears when he threatened me with "one last chance" before I was booted off the Constant Contact system.

**cardcommunications**

There's no excuse for the person on the phone to be rude to you.

HOWEVER, Constant Contact is just protecting their integrity—because . . . every spam complaint to every account is potentially a blacklist from an ISP.

If you find another email service provider who isn't so concerned about spam complaints— I would worry about them—because it's possible their mail is ending up in spam folders everywhere or just downright blocked by ISPs.

I would suggest [fine-tuning] your permission reminder and [writing] it as specifically as possible (i.e., you are receiving this email because you filled out a request for info form on our website and asked to receive email communications from us).

If you gained permission in a shady way (i.e., not explicitly asking for permission) then you should re-think your email marketing strategy!

Take a look at what Kelly is doing for Constant Contact. If BadAndy 80 got his list without asking people's permission, he'll give up on Constant Contact, taking his bad reputation with him. If he's just made a mistake, she's educated him and he might change how he does business. And for anybody else who reads this exchange, she's educated *them*. She's helped Constant Contact improve the behavior and integrity of its customer base, an asset that helps *all* its customers prevent being perceived as spammers. And education in the community is a heck of a lot cheaper than shutting people off.

As Maureen says, "It's about making them feel like a stakeholder. If they really feel that way, they are a part of our success. Who would leave Constant Contact when they feel that way?"

## *Lessons from Energizing a Community*

What can you take away from Constant Contact's experience with its community?

First, business-to-business companies have an advantage in building communities. Businesspeople form communities around their roles—in this case, as email marketers in small businesses. In fact, all of a company's business customers are far more likely to feel they have something in common than a consumer company's customers—because they're all trying to get the same work done. Consumer companies' customers may feel this affinity (like Mini owners), or they may not (like eBags' luggage customers).

Second, communities can get out of hand. Gail and Maureen watched the first spam discussions with increasing alarm. To their credit, they took action and turned the community's attitude around to their advantage. Don't start a community until you've thought through what you'll do if conflicts like this arise. (And shutting off community members who say negative things isn't an option—they may well set up camp in a private community where you've got no influence over them at all.)

Finally, be sure you know what your objectives are going in. Constant Contact's community was designed from the start to energize customers. All the activity in the community (like the "show off your best campaign" section that's just begun) is about re-inforcing positive behaviors, encouraging new customers, and generating referrals. This means Gail and Maureen can measure their success—a critical element of real groundswell thinking.

## Case Study

### Lego: Energizing an Existing Community

Some products develop such enthusiastic supporters that communities spring up naturally.

Ask Tormod Askildsen. He's the senior director of business development at the Lego Group, the sixth-largest toy manufacturer in the world. But his job is to help sell Lego sets to people who don't see Lego as a toy at all.

Tormod is aiming at Lego buyers who think it's a creative building material, not just a toy. These are the adult fans of Lego, or AFOLs, whom he says are responsible for 5 percent to 10 percent of Lego's billion-dollar-plus business.

For example, in 2005 Lego created a product that seemed a little crazy at the time. The Imperial Star Destroyer kit costs $299 and includes 3,104 pieces. And once launched, it started flying off the shelves, becoming one of the most popular Lego kits ever. Who was buying these huge kits? Mostly grown-ups.

Tormod Askildsen was well aware of the AFOLs' own vibrant community, LUGNET, the International Lego Users Group Network (www.lugnet.com), which is not owned or operated by Lego. LUGNET is a global community of thousands of Lego enthusiasts. For Lego, replicating LUGNET on its own site would be a prescription for failure. Remember, community is about people's needs to connect, not your need to control, so if they're already out there, respect that.

Instead, Lego created a program called Lego Ambassadors. The Lego Ambassadors program accomplishes two goals: it builds relationships with the most enthusiastic AFOLs, and it helps Lego learn what's going on out in the highly connected AFOL world. Lego Ambassadors get information from the company on products coming out and then spread that information to their own personal networks, both in person and online. And the Lego Ambassadors have an explicit responsibility to listen to other AFOLs, develop consensus, and highlight their desires to the Lego company.

Active Lego builders vie to become one of the twenty-five or so ambassadors chosen by Lego. By limiting the number of positions, the Lego company creates competition, energizing its fans to step up and become spokespeople for the company's message. And Lego Ambassadors aren't paid in cash; they're paid in Lego bricks! That kind of compensation is cheap for the company yet highly valued by the ambassadors.

### The ROI of Energizing a Community

What's it worth to Tormod Askildsen to energize the existing community of Lego enthusiasts? A whole lot more than it costs, that's for sure.

Lego Ambassadors require only Internet coordination, staff time, some travel, and payment in Lego bricks. We'd estimate the cost of a program like this at around $200,000.

But Tormod's twenty-five Lego Ambassadors are in touch with around a hundred other people each, more if you count their interactions online. That's around twenty-five hundred AFOLs, each of whom might be buying $1,000 of Lego products a year. If that increases to $1,200 a year based on the ambassadors' efforts, the company has used a $200,000 investment to increase sales by $500,000.

As with eBags, there's another return that's more subtle. The ambassadors bring Lego feedback on its products. They represent the community to the company. Because the AFOL community is so tightly knit and interdependent, the Lego Ambassador program means that Tormod and the product designers at Lego have an immediate two-way connection to the most influential members of that community. And as you may have read in *Wired*, Lego has even included these active customers in product design discussions. This has incalculable value in helping ensure that products designed for adult Lego buyers will actually succeed. In this case, energizing the base includes a strong element of listening as well.

## How You Energize Depends on How You Want Relationships to Change

The examples in this chapter show three good ways to energize your customers—with ratings and reviews, communities, and ambassador programs. But there are many more, depending on what your customer base is like—and how you hope to change your relationship with those customers.

For example, Fiskars, a company that makes scissors and scrapbooking supplies, worked with a consultancy called Brains On Fire to create an ambassador program like Lego's. The program includes a community like Constant Contact's at www.fiskateers.com. After an intensive search, Fiskars picked four ambassadors who have now become icons in the scrapbooking community. Fiskars pays its ambassadors, but they return far more value in getting women charged up about scrapbooking.

Carnival Cruise Lines developed a program that helps people plan cruises with friends. Once you sign up at www.carnivalconnections.com, you can use the tools there to connect with friends, invite them along, and coordinate activities. Given the sporadic nature of Carnival's customer base, this event-based energizing strategy makes sense.

These companies were smart—they considered the propensities of their customer bases first, then designed strategies and chose technologies that matched the relationships they already had, and provided ways for their customers to extend those relationships. Do this skillfully, and you can get your customers to sell each other, too.

## Advice for Energizers

Energizing is both more powerful and riskier than the techniques we discussed in the previous two chapters on listening and talking. The reason? Now you're dealing with *people* who are going to talk about your brand. As much as companies say they're in touch with their customers' needs, dealing with actual customers creates challenges for which they're often not ready.

If you want to energize your customers, you must prepare for a new way of thinking. Here are five steps for applying the techniques of energizing to your own organization.

## 1. Figure Out if You Want to Energize the Groundswell

Energizing works well for companies with customers who are, or could be, enthusiastic about the company and its products. It's not for everybody.

Some companies provide commodities like copier paper or memory chips to their customers, products that are available from multiple suppliers and don't have strong brands or emotional connections. If this is your business, fine, but don't assume your customers want to talk about your products. Other companies succeed despite a significant number of dissatisfied customers. If that's you, then energizing your customers will only make things worse. If you're in either of these situations, we recommend listening to the groundswell so you can learn more about your customers' attitudes.

Even for companies with enthusiastic customers, energizing the groundswell can be bracing. The good news is that you'll connect, directly, to what people are really thinking. That's the bad news, too. Think about Jim Noble and his laptop bag or AFOLs with their Lego trains. Do you really want to hear from these folks? Do you want your other customers to hear from them? Unless you and your whole management team can answer with an unequivocal yes, then you might not be ready to energize the groundswell.

## 2. Check the Social Profile of Your Customers

You need research to determine how actively and in what numbers your customers are participating in the groundswell. If you're selling PDAs or baseball mitts—anything that skews young and technologically savvy—then your customers are already heavily into the groundswell, and you can expect them to take naturally to a collection of community and social features. If you're selling mattresses or estate planning, then rein in your expectations accordingly—it's no use starting a community if your best customers have the wrong profile and won't be participating.

## 3. Ask Yourself, "What Is My Customer's Problem?"

Remember, except in rare cases like Lego's, communities don't form around your products. If you have trouble believing this, just remember Procter & Gamble's beinggirl.com community, which was built around girls' problems, not feminine care products. Even Lego's customers aren't really talking about

Legos; they're talking about *building* with Legos, which isn't quite the same thing. As eBags takes the next step, it might learn that its customers' problems center around travel in general, not just luggage.

## 4. Pick a Strategy That Fits Your Customers' Social Profile and Problems

For retailers and other direct sellers, ratings and reviews make sense and have a proven payoff. If a lot of your customers like to react to online content, this is a great place to start.

For other companies, communities make sense. But check first. If your customers already have communities, like Lego's, then it's best to participate in those communities rather than build your own.

But be prepared. Although there are free community tools available from companies like ning.com and KickApps, to make a community that's successful, you must consider the costs of design, moderation, and marketing, which can easily run into the hundreds of thousands of dollars.

## 5. Don't Start Unless You Can Stick Around for the Long Haul

A community is like a marriage; it requires constant adjustment to grow and become more rewarding. And if you're not in it for the long haul, well, maybe you should think about the ugly endings you've seen to marriages that lacked that long-term effort.

Think about eBags' ratings. If the company stopped them, or stopped supporting them, not only would the site become stale and less popular, but the energized customers would suffer a backlash. Jim Noble is not a guy you want to antagonize; he'll start telling people how great eBags *used* to be before it stopped listening to people like him. If Lego stopped connecting with its top AFOLs, their enthusiasm would fade and the community would shrink.

## How Energizing Will Transform Your Company

In energizing the groundswell, you'll find out that not all your customers are equal.

In this chapter we talk about energizing the base. The base includes your most enthusiastic customers. But just like the base that any politician depends on, the base expects something back. It expects you to listen.

Whether you're anointing brand ambassadors like Lego, inviting customers into a community like Constant Contact, or empowering people with reviews like eBags, you're going to unleash some powerful voices.

Lego explicitly acknowledges that its brand ambassador program goes both ways—it is dependent on the brand ambassadors for ideas about future products and ways of doing business. In a comparable way, eBags has put Jim Noble on its advisory panel and checks in with him on ideas for its products. And eBags also taps its best reviewers to be field testers, sending them bags for review to get a preview of how the larger audience might like—or reject—those bags.

What happens if community members turn against you? If the top poster on LUGNET started dissing Lego's management or a group of Constant Contact's community members insisted on a change in policy, these companies would have an imperative to listen. An energized community expects a response, and energized customers wield power within the community of customers. The message, for any company, is to listen and, whenever possible, to give customers what they desire most.

What they want is information about the company's present and future products. They also want to see evidence that they are making a difference. A company that starts by energizing the groundswell will end up with a whole bunch of unpaid R&D partners. So long as you're willing to engage with your enthusiasts, this is fine. But they're yours forever—you can't lay them off if they stop behaving the way you want.

This is why companies that start out by energizing their most enthusiastic customers often end up *embracing* them—that is, turning those customers into an integral part of the company's products and processes. Including customers in the product development process and as extensions of your business is exciting, but once again, the groundswell leads you to a space where you're less and less in control of your own business and brand.

# Notes

## Listening to the Groundswell

1. *Here's a comment from "Tracy D" in the Communispace forum:* This quote comes from NCCN's private community of cancer patients managed by Communispace. Since this community is proprietary to NCCN, it's not available for viewing without a password. We gratefully acknowledge Communispace and NCCN for allowing us to review and quote from this community. The remainder of the quotes from cancer patients in this chapter comes from this community.

2. *Mini owners scored well above average on community activities, like sharing pictures and joining local clubs. Here's a typical comment:* This quote and subsequent quotes from Mini owners come from the presentation "MINI WOMMA Case Study: Managing & Galvanizing Brand Community," presented by Ed Cotton of Butler, Shine, Stern & Partners and Mark Witthoefft of MotiveQuest in May 2007.

## Talking with the Groundswell

1. *And since 74 percent of college students are members of social networks:* All adult consumer statistics in this chapter come from Forrester's North American Social Technographics Online Survey, Q2 2007.

2. *According to Market Evolution—a consultancy that analyzed the campaign for MySpace and Carat in a 2007 report called "Never Ending*

# Notes

*Friending"*: "Never Ending Friending" has its own MySpace page at www.myspace.com/neverendingfriending. The PDF of the report is available at groundswell.forrester.com/site6-9.

## Energizing the Groundswell

1. Fred Reichheld estimates the value of each promoter's positive word of mouth at $42: See *The Ultimate Question: Driving Good Profits and True Growth* by Fred Reichheld (Boston: Harvard Business School Press, 2006), pp. 50–54.

# Index

# Index

# Index

# Index

# Index

# Index

# Index

# About the Authors

**Charlene Li**, formerly of Forrester Research, is an independent thought leader and founder of the Altimeter Group.

**Josh Bernoff**, Senior Vice President, Idea Development at Forrester Research, is one of America's most frequently quoted research analysts.